John Patrick Byrne
A Big Adventure

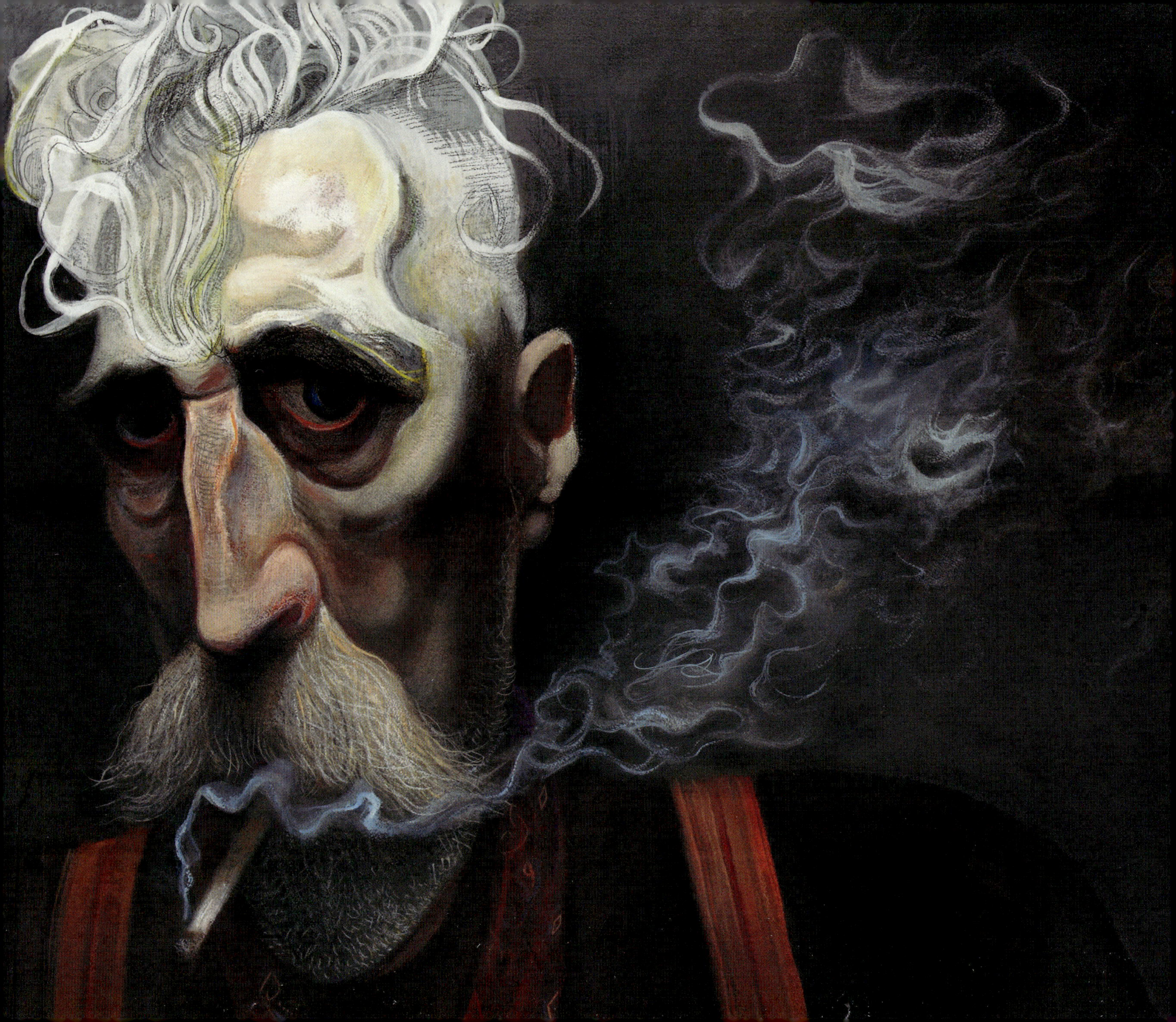

John Patrick Byrne
A Big Adventure

Martin McSheaffrey-Craig

Glasgow Museums Publishing

First published in 2022 by Glasgow Museums Publishing, part of Glasgow Life, to accompany the exhibition *John Byrne: A Big Adventure. Artist, Writer and Theatre Maker*, 27 May–18 September 2022, Kelvingrove Art Gallery and Museum, Glasgow, Scotland.

Images of John Byrne's artwork are © John Byrne. All rights reserved. DACS 2022. All images reproduced with the lenders' kind permission. Thanks to The Fine Art Society for assistance in sourcing images.
Photograph of John Byrne p. 7: © David Eustace, reproduced by kind permission.
Pig's Head (Perugia) p.19, image courtesy of The Hunterian
Jock and the Tiger Cat p.25, reproduced courtesy of Perth Museum & Art Gallery, Perth & Kinross Council
Photograph of John Byrne painting the dome of the King's Theatre, Edinburgh, p.28, © Ron O'Donnell, courtesy of Capital Theatres
National Velvet, p.39, and *The Studio*, pp.70–71, images © Copyright of OneRen, the trading name of Renfrewshire Leisure Limited
The Slab Boys stage performance, p.46, photo by Martha Swope ©The New York Public Library for the Performing Arts
Donald Meets the Devildogs, p.59, *Drunken Sailor*, p.67, and *Harlequin with Guitar*, p.89, reproduced courtesy of Glasgow Print Studio
Self Portrait in Flowered Jacket, p.68; *Billy Connolly, Entertainer*, p.78; *Red and Unread*, p.79, images © National Galleries Scotland, www.nationalgalleries.org
Rebecca, p.82, image courtesy The Fine Art Society/John McKenzie Photography
Celie Asleep, p.83, courtesy of City Art Centre, Museums & Galleries Edinburgh
Say it With Flowers, p.91, © Andy Phillipson/livewireimage.com, courtesy of The Fine Art Society

Every effort has been made to trace copyright holders and to acknowledge the correct copyright of images. Any errors or omissions are unintentional and should be brought to the publisher's attention, who will arrange for corrections to appear in any reprints.

Text copyright: © Culture and Sport Glasgow (Museums); Emily Walsh's foreword © The Fine Art Society

ISBN 978-1-908638-41-0

Designed by Caroline and Roger Hillier, The Old Chapel Graphic Design
Edited by Susan Pacitti; Research Manager: Rebecca Quinton
Photography of Glasgow Museums' works by Glasgow Museums Photography Section; additional photography of lenders' works by
Jim Dunn; Billy Connolly mural in situ by Enzo di Cosmo

Printed in Scotland by J Thomson Colour Printers, Glasgow
Cover printed on 350gsm Galerie Art Silk; text printed on 150gsm Galerie Art Silk

FSC
MIX
Paper from responsible sources
www.fsc.org
FSC® C023105

Front cover: *Hands Up*, 2006, oil on board, frame painted by John Byrne, 149cm × 118cm, lent by Andrew and Fiona Paterson
Back cover: *Portrait of Gerry Rafferty*, painted guitar, about 1970, Martin D-35 acoustic guitar, paint, 103.5cm × 39.6cm × 13cm, lent by Martha Rafferty
Frontispiece: detail from *Big Selfie*, 2014, casein on paper, 137cm × 112cm, purchased in 2014 by the late Angus Crichton-Miller
p. 96: *John Byrne* signature, acrylic on board, 28cm × 38cm, private collection, Charles Marks

Note: all dimensions given are framed sizes, unless otherwise noted.

Contents

Acknowledgements

Glasgow Museums would like to thank:

John and Jeanine Byrne, and their family and friends who have kindly supported this exhibition.

The Fine Art Society, in particular Emily Walsh and Camilla Riva.

Everyone who was kind enough to agree to be interviewed for the exhibition.

The John Byrne Award, for the use of their logo at the entrance to the exhibition.

A very special thank you to all the private and institutional lenders, without whom this exhibition and publication would not be possible, and to the organizations that supplied supporting material for the exhibition.

Portrait of John Byrne by David Eustace

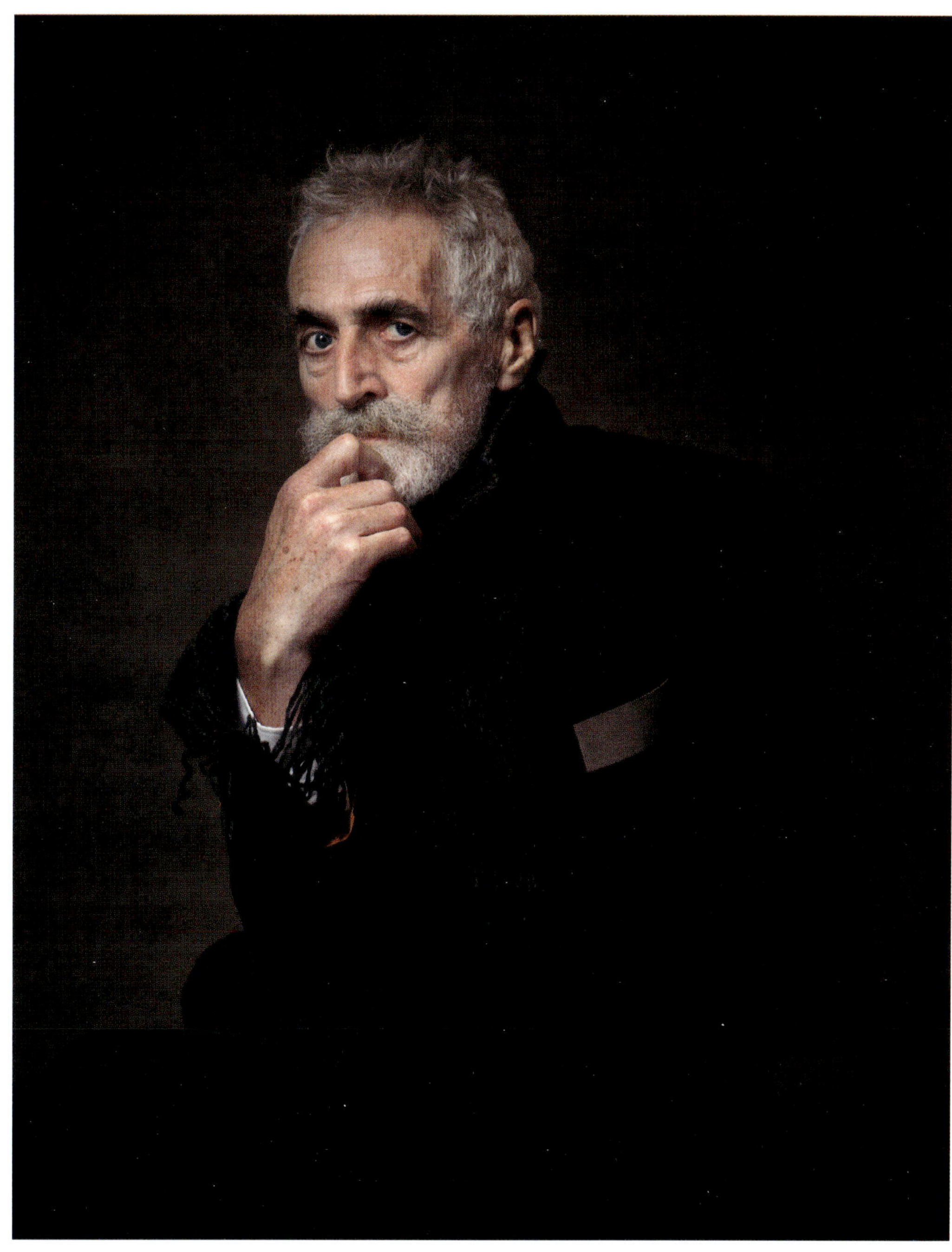

Foreword

I am delighted that we have been able to stage this retrospective at Kelvingrove Art Gallery and Museum, the first major exhibition of John Byrne's work for several years. Although Glasgow cannot claim Byrne as its own, as he was born in Paisley, and now lives in Edinburgh, he is very much entwined with the west of Scotland and has had a significant cultural influence. Over the years his career has been nothing if not eclectic, from his distinctive style of art to award-winning plays and television dramas – he is a master storyteller.

When we first started planning this exhibition, I was always mindful that I wanted the substantial number of works by Byrne in Glasgow Museums' collection to sit at the heart of the exhibition. These include the famous portrait of Byrne's friend Billy Connolly. As a result of curator Martin McSheaffrey-Craig's work with John to develop the exhibition, I think I can safely say that we now have a far greater understanding of both Byrne's work in general, and the works in our collection.

The exhibition showcases John Patrick Byrne's work not just as an artist, but also as a writer, playwright, screen writer and set and costume designer, and we are very grateful to all those lenders, both private and institutional, who have been so generous in lending works to allow us to illustrate the breadth of his talents. We are also very grateful to John himself, and to his wife Jeanine, for being so generous with their time and giving us an insight into his work and practice.

This exhibition has been made possible as a result of the Government Indemnity Scheme. Glasgow Life would like to thank HM Government for providing Government Indemnity and the Department for Digital, Culture, Media and Sport and Arts Council England for arranging the indemnity.

Duncan Dornan
Head of Museums and Collections, Glasgow Life

Preface

'"Paisley Buddies" are, to a man and a woman, total oddballs. I should know, I'm one of them', said John once. I was in my early 20s when I first met him. I'd known about John Byrne at school (and my parents had parrotted *Tutti Frutti* throughout my teens). I'd studied him at university. Then I was asked to pick up actual paintings from the man himself. My admiration and awe at his facility have remained undimmed. John himself, though unquestionably a star, has always been kind and warm. I'm lucky to know him.

Knowing him, though, cuts two ways. There is the blethering and reminiscing over cups of black tea. Then there are the pictures. In the decades since he left The Glasgow School of Art, he has accumulated through his work an extensive pictorial autobiography. Paintings of 1950s' Ferguslie Park – Feegie – captured what was once an invention, the 'teenager'. Thereafter, drawing on his apprenticeship at AF Stoddard & Co. in Paisley (a 'Technicolour hell hole', he called it) as a 'slab boy', much of what was to come, visually and literally, drew on what John observed there.

In his *Underwood Lane* series, the Teddy Boys who loiter are reminiscences of his past. Filmic and theatrical worlds are referenced, backdrops lit like stage sets. Nocturnal themes abound: moonlit woods; the streets of 1950s' Paisley; the self-examining artist, alone and wreathed in cigarette smoke. In a finely balanced act, he pulls together the macabre and humourous.

From the early 1970s, John diversified into writing, designing and directing stage and screen productions. Perhaps because of the immense success of these productions his prodigious talent as an artist was temporarily overshadowed. He didn't stop, however, but continued instead to design theatre sets and costumes. To appreciate his hunger to write, draw and paint is overwhelming for the onlooker. For the artist it's unstoppable.

John's a well-kent face by dint of his many self portraits. His finely cultivated appearance and hooded, often sleep-deprived, eyes look out and kid us into an intimacy with him. His image serves to distract us from what John is chasing in his elusive self.

Which brings us back to oddballs: running through all of John's work is the outsider, either as a lone figure or a fragment of society. Oddity is seen through a prism of the fantastic and John makes magic of it.

Emily Walsh
The Fine Art Society

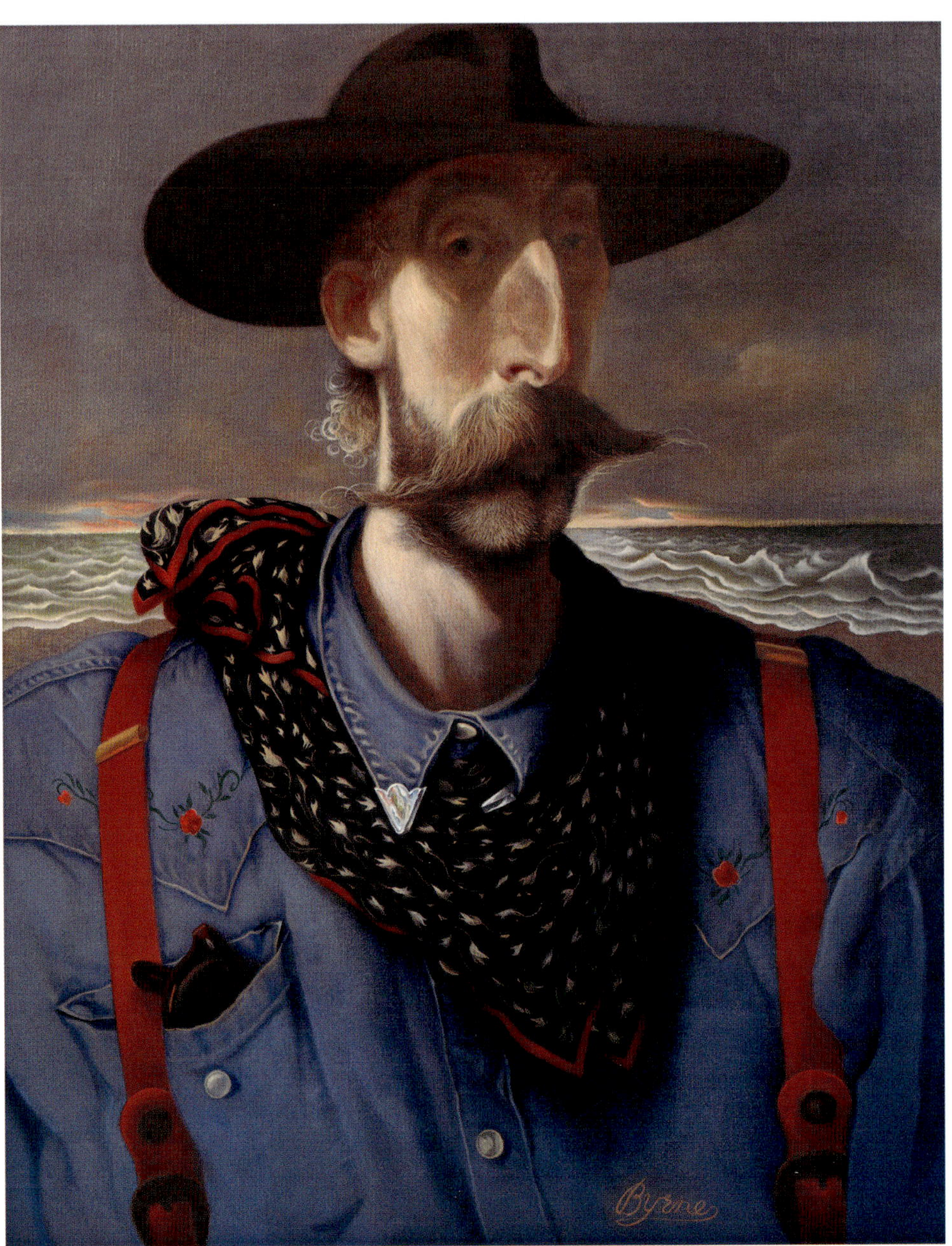

Self Portrait in Stetson 1989
Oil on canvas
91.5cm × 72cm (unframed)
Bought by Glasgow Museums 1991
3469

Introduction

Born in Paisley in 1940, John Patrick Byrne defies attempts to label him. This artist, playwright and theatre maker has created many a character and world, often inspired by his hometown of Paisley and early years there. A polymath and cultural icon, in 2004 he was made an associate of the Royal Scottish Academy and a full member in 2007. Byrne is an Honorary Fellow of The Glasgow School of Art and the Royal Incorporation of Architects in Scotland, an Honorary Member of the Royal Glasgow Institute of the Fine Arts, and has honorary doctorates from the Universities of Paisley, Glasgow, Aberdeen and Strathclyde. In 2001, he returned his MBE in protest over the Iraq War.

You may recognize his distinctive style, moustachioed and bearded, cigarette in hand. Or his portraits of his friends such as Billy Connolly, or the album covers he designed for musicians Gerry Rafferty, Donovan, The Beatles, that have sold millions around the world.

It is more than likely you will know him as the writer of *The Slab Boys*, a play which critic Joyce McMillan credits with changing Scottish theatre, saying of it that 'The opening of John Byrne's *Slab Boys* in 1978 was perhaps the key moment when Scottish theatre leapt decisively from the reproduction of various established traditions or representations of Scotland... it was the point when it finally became clear that Scottishness was not a dying or fading culture, but a thriving, chaotic, ever-changing post-modern one with a future as well as a past.' This series of plays has endured, not only providing a launchpad for the careers of actors such as Kevin Bacon, Robbie Coltrane, Alan Cumming, Gerard Kelly, Val Kilmer and Sean Penn, but making its way onto the education curriculum.

If you are of a certain age you will certainly remember the dramas he wrote for the BBC, *Tutti Frutti* (1987) and *Your Cheatin' Heart* (1990), watched avidly by millions weekly, and which have now become cult classics. Who can fail to remember Robbie Coltrane as Danny McGlone, Emma Thompson as Suzie Kettles, Maurice Roeves as Vincent Diver, or Richard Wilson as Eddie Clockerty, reprimanding 'Miss Toner' (Katy Murphy) yet again?

But Byrne's first love has always been painting. Graduating from The Glasgow School of Art in 1963, with multiple awards, the expectations of greatness – he was described by one lecturer as 'unquestionably one of the most able painters we have seen in the past 20 years' – were not fulfilled as easily as predicted. To find true success Byrne had to create a character based loosely on his father, the artist Patrick.

Fame as an artist did follow, even after he stopped signing his paintings 'Patrick', and his works are in collections and institutions around the world. However, some might say that Byrne's talent and impact as an artist have never truly been recognized; his plays are written about more than his art is. Ironically, this under-representation of his artwork could be because between 1975 and 1992 Byrne stopped exhibiting and concentrated on his plays. He has never stopped painting though; indeed, he has produced so much work that a comprehensive retrospective would have filled the Kelvingrove exhibition gallery many times over. However, I hope that I have managed to capture at least a flavour of the diversity and energy of Byrne's career, celebrating why he is a true Scottish cultural icon.

Martin McSheaffrey Craig
Curator of Art Post-1945

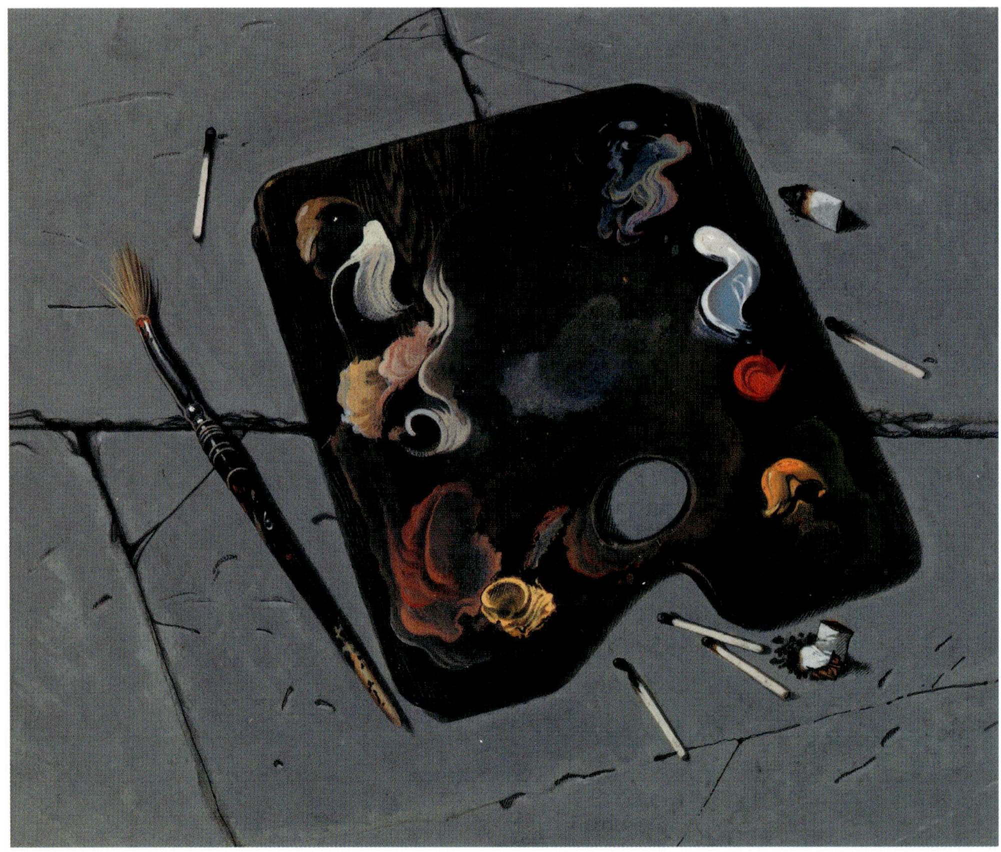

Palette, Dowts and Matches 1975
Watercolour; gouache
24.7cm × 28.5cm (unframed)
Bought by Glasgow Museums, 1994
PR.1994.1

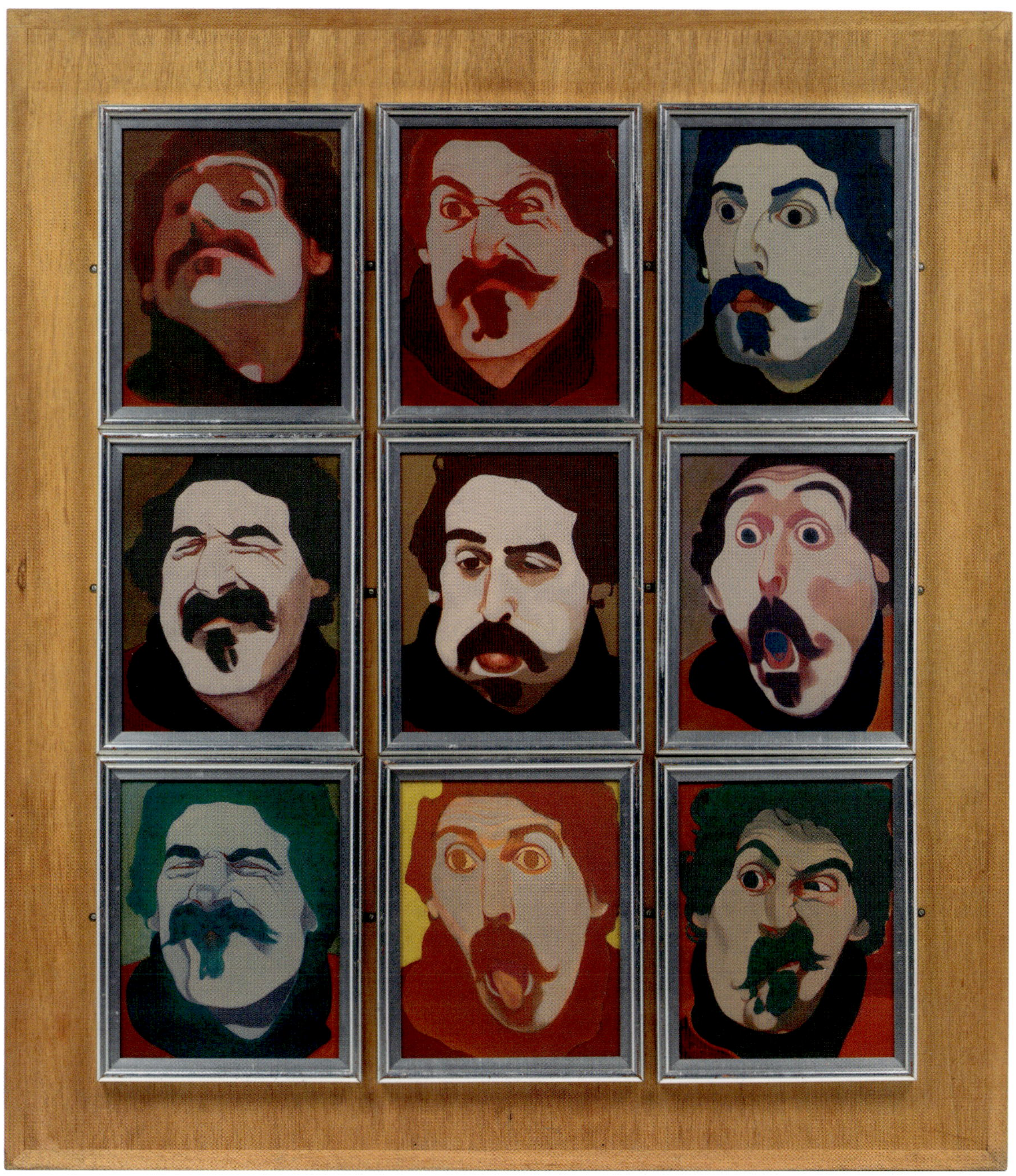

To Be Continued
1975
Acrylic on wood panel
120cm × 100cm
(unframed)
Bought by Glasgow
Museums, 1976
3334

Early years

Byrne was born and raised in Ferguslie Park, Paisley, then one of the most deprived areas in Europe. Despite this, he speaks of it as being a very positive experience, providing 'the grit in the oyster that makes the pearl', and growing up in 'a house full of love' was an affirming, positive experience.

The Catholic faith Byrne was brought up in has remained central to Byrne's beliefs, echoed constantly in his art and writing – he says it is 'within his DNA'.

He was named John, but for a while was known by the pet name 'Ian', the Gaelic form of the name, as a tribute to the Highland midwife who had delivered him. Byrne talks of visiting the library and museum as a boy with his dad, who would tell him stories of his travels round the world and how he had shot Buddy, Paisley Museum's famous and beloved taxidermy lion, with one of the guns also on display. However, in later years when the displays changed but the story did not, Byrne realized that his dad had been making these stories up, though he never told him that.

After he left school (St Mirin's Academy), Byrne worked at Paisley carpet factory AF Stoddard & Co. as a slab boy, mixing colours for the carpet designers. He would later draw on this as inspiration for his play of the same name. Dreams of going to art school and making his own mark became reality in 1958, when he got into the prestigious Glasgow School of Art. However, Byrne struggled to find himself there, having to re-sit his first year, then transferring to Edinburgh Art School after his general course, only to transfer back to Glasgow. Although he was a favourite of his tutors, and clearly very talented, his interest in figurative painting went against the fashion of the day. (This trait, of going against the establishment and choosing his own path, is one that Byrne has continued throughout his career.)

Despite this, Byrne flourished, going on to win the Newberry Medal for best final year student, and the Bellahouston Travelling Scholarship. This allowed him to travel to Italy, where he studied in Perugia between 1963 and 1964.

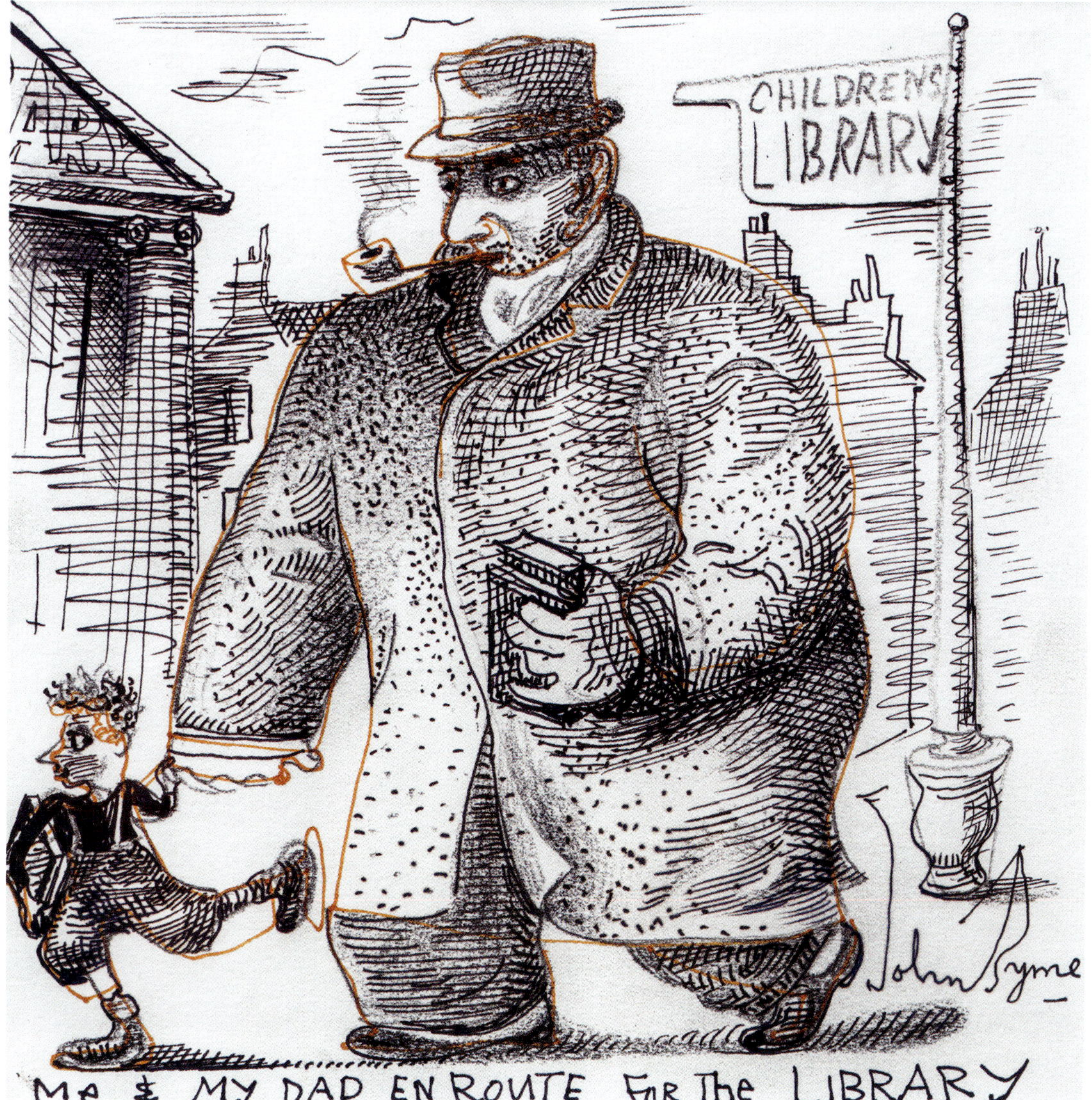

Me and My Dad En Route for the Library, 2017
Ink and graphite on paper
39.5cm × 41.3cm
Lent by Adriano Martinelli

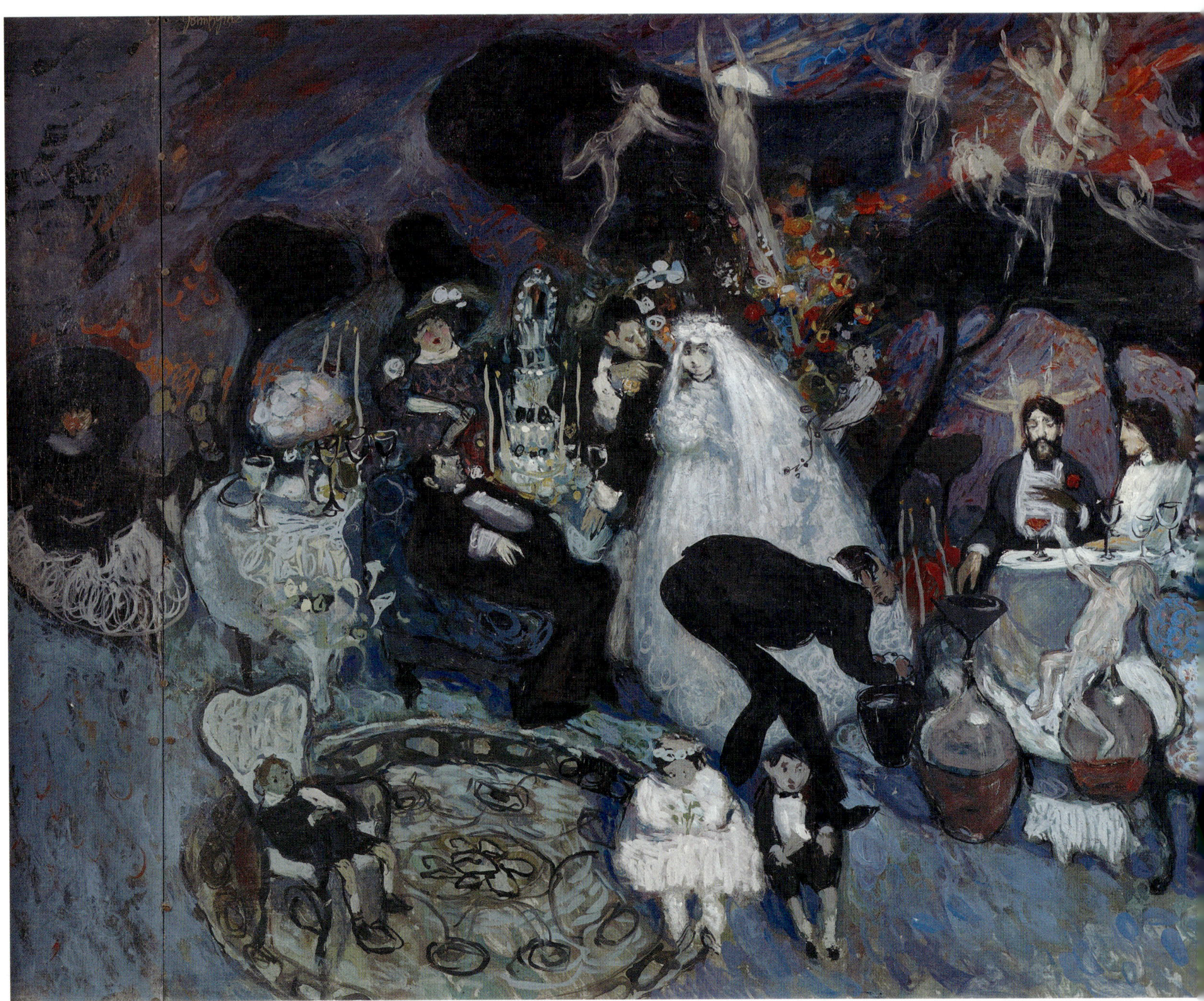

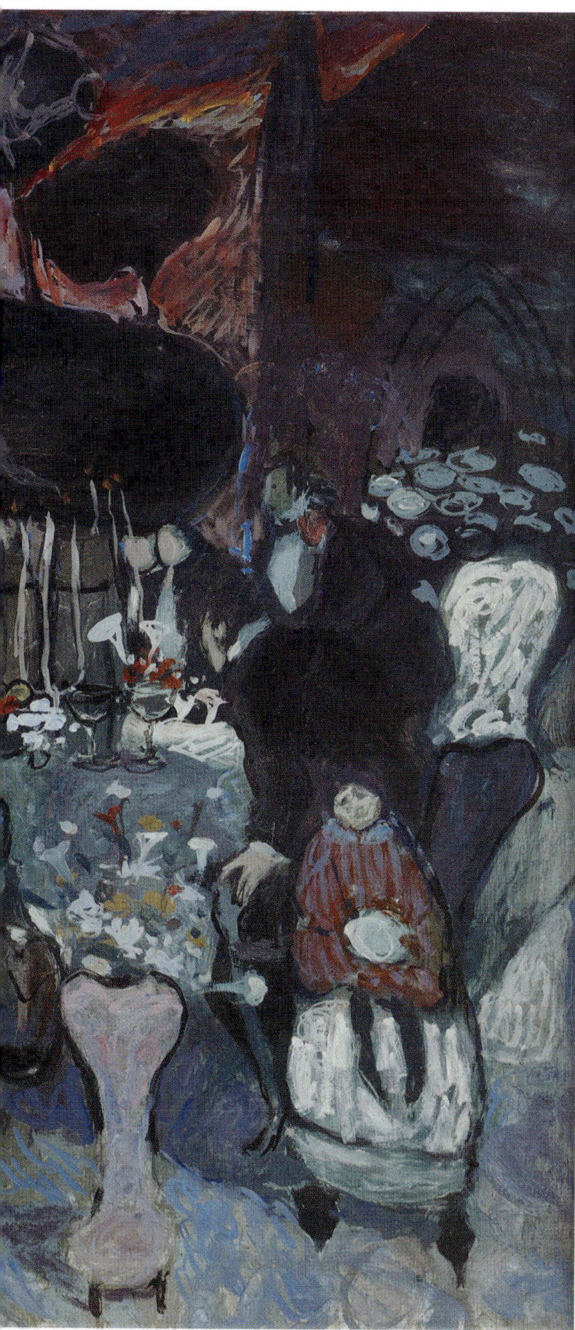

The Marriage at Cana, about 1962
Oil on canvas
78cm × 118cm
Lent by Carole and David Warren

In a set exercise for a tutor at art school, Byrne placed this biblical story from the gospel of St John (of Jesus turning water into wine at a wedding) in an Edwardian setting with naked angels. The painting is beautiful and complex, with bold brush work playing the perspective and composition. However, although he was a supporter of Byrne's work, The Glasgow School of Art Director Douglas Percy Bliss called the painting blasphemous.

The Mark, 2002
Pen on paper
50cm × 50cm
Private Collection, Charles Marks

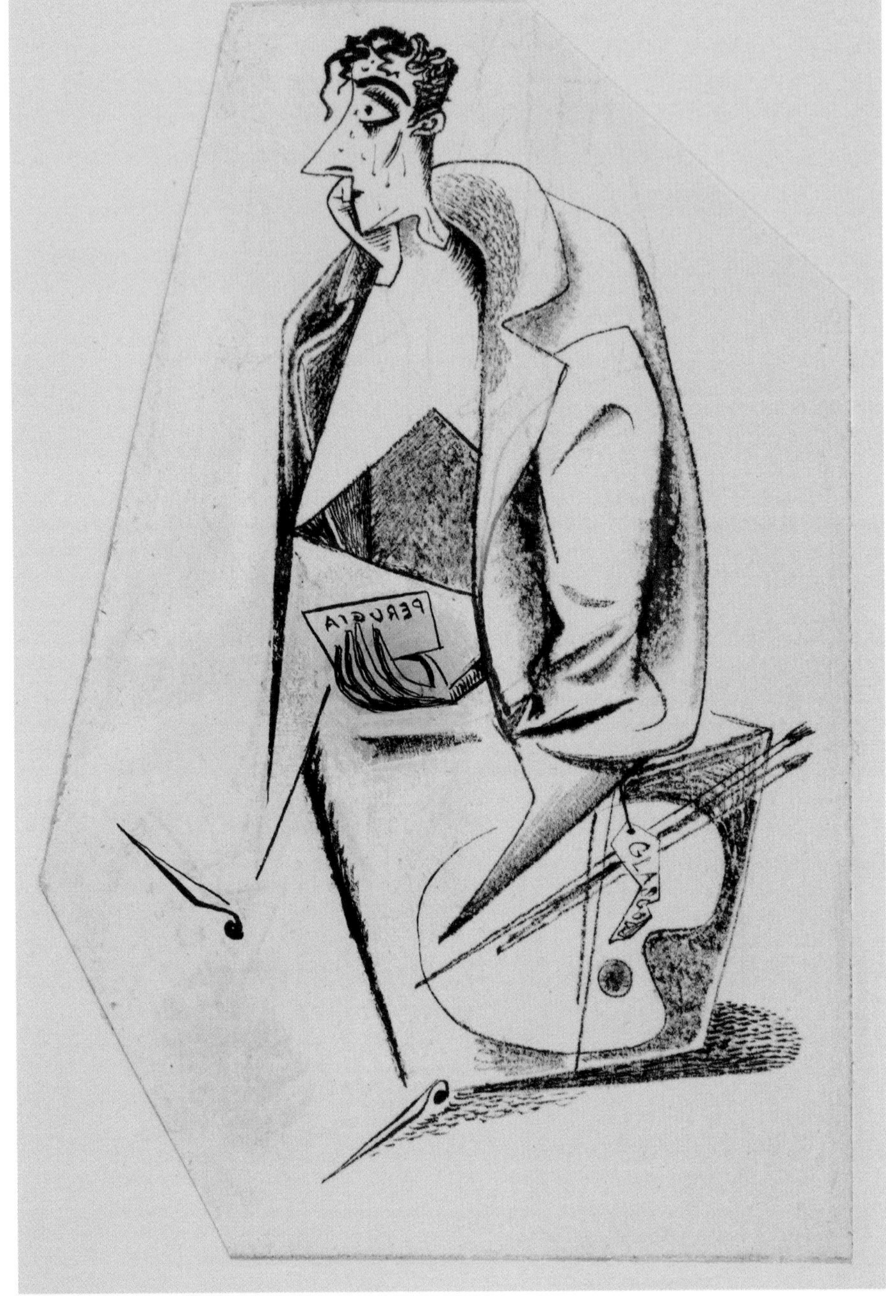

This Cubist-style drawing sees Byrne
depicting himself as 'The Mark' – he was
conned out of money while travelling in
Italy on a scholarship in 1963.

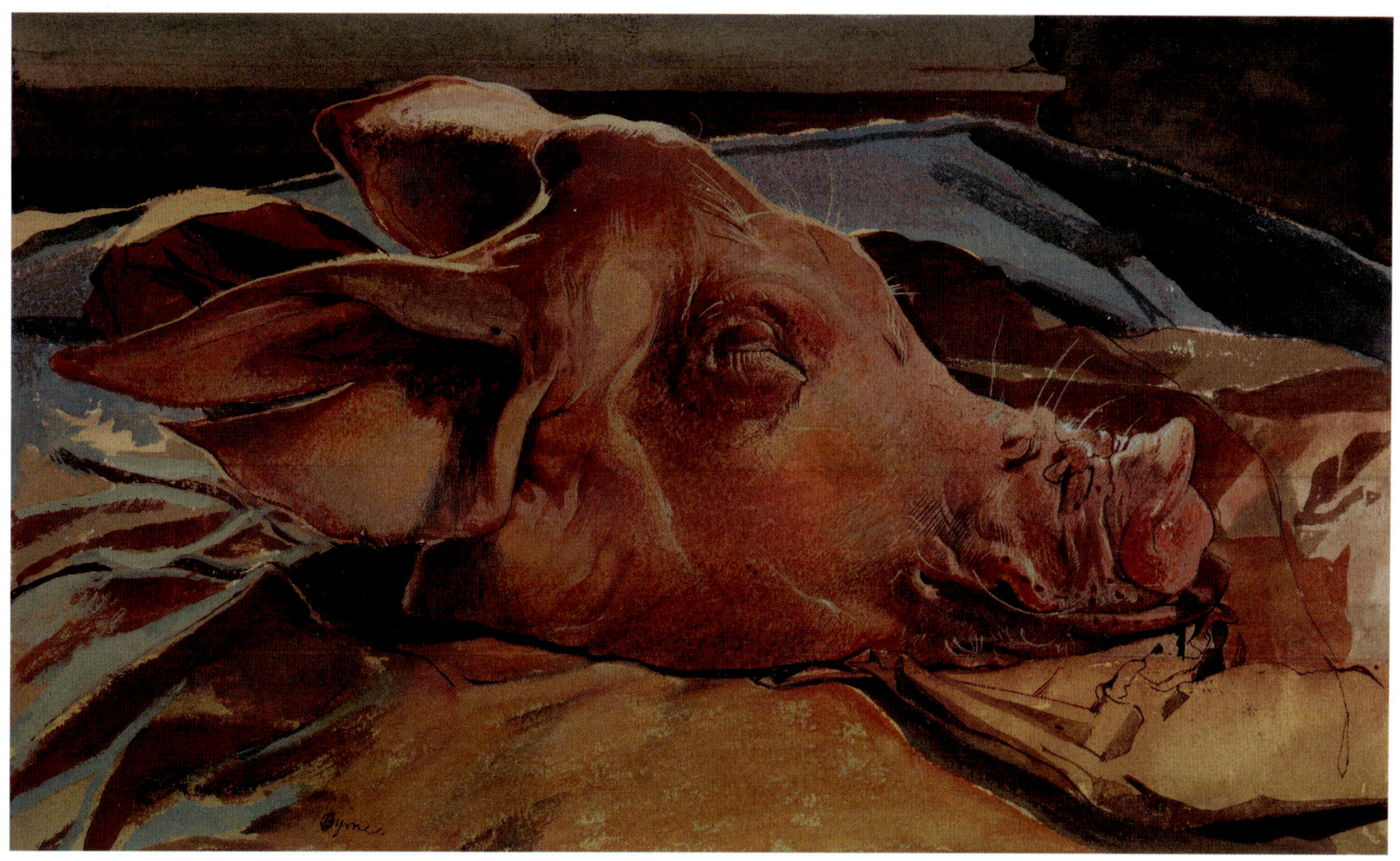

Pig's Head (Perugia), 1964
Watercolour pen and pencil on paper
47.4cm × 62.5cm
The Hunterian, University of Glasgow,
GLAHA 42057

This was done when Byrne was studying in Perugia, on the Bellahouston Travelling Scholarship. In a letter to Douglas Percy Bliss, Director of The Glasgow School of Art, Byrne said that he found this 'very exciting and enjoyed the work very much although at first I felt a little queasy'.

Patrick

The American Boy, 1971
Signed as Patrick
Oil on board
216cm × 246cm (unframed)
Bought by Glasgow Museums, 1992
3495

Arguably Byrne's most ambitious Patrick painting, the large scale meant it did not get sold when it was first made. The painting was so large Byrne had to cut it in half with a saw and store it under the floorboards in his house.

On his return to Scotland, Byrne married and by 1965 had two children, John Francis and Melanie Cecilia. With a family to support, he started work as a graphic designer for STV, then returned to AF Stoddard & Co. as a carpet designer, teaching evening classes at The Glasgow School of Art, and designing book covers for Penguin Books to make ends meet. He continued to paint in his garage, but his aim to be a full-time artist seemed impossible without moving to London. An article by Barrie Sturt-Penrose in a supplement to the *Observer* newspaper in 1966, which discussed the interest in 'primitive' or 'naïve' artists, describing them as 'inevitably ordinary working men who begin painting solely for their own pleasure and without any art training', gave him an idea. Byrne certainly painted for pleasure, but had five years of art school training, so he decided to send a small painting in a 'primitive' style of a man with a flower to London's Portal Gallery, which had featured in the article, pretending it was the work of his father. Blending information from his own and his father's lives, he created an alter ego, the artist Patrick. The gallery loved the work, asked for more, and then offered 'Patrick' a solo exhibition. Before its opening, Byrne confessed that it had been a ruse. Luckily, the gallery took it well and the exhibition was a sell-out.

The initial early Patrick works are simplistic, but once freed from pretending to be his father, Byrne's Patrick work developed rapidly. 'Patrick' has a flat graphic style that can be read easily, but once you start looking more closely, you see sophisticated brushwork, composition and ideas. There has been conjecture that Patrick was just a means to an end, not Byrne's true style, but it is more complicated than that.

In his confessional letter to the Portal Gallery Byrne said 'When I was doing the paintings I didn't slip into a mantle and assume a style alien to my own. I felt at home.' To this day, he still signs some paintings 'Patrick'.

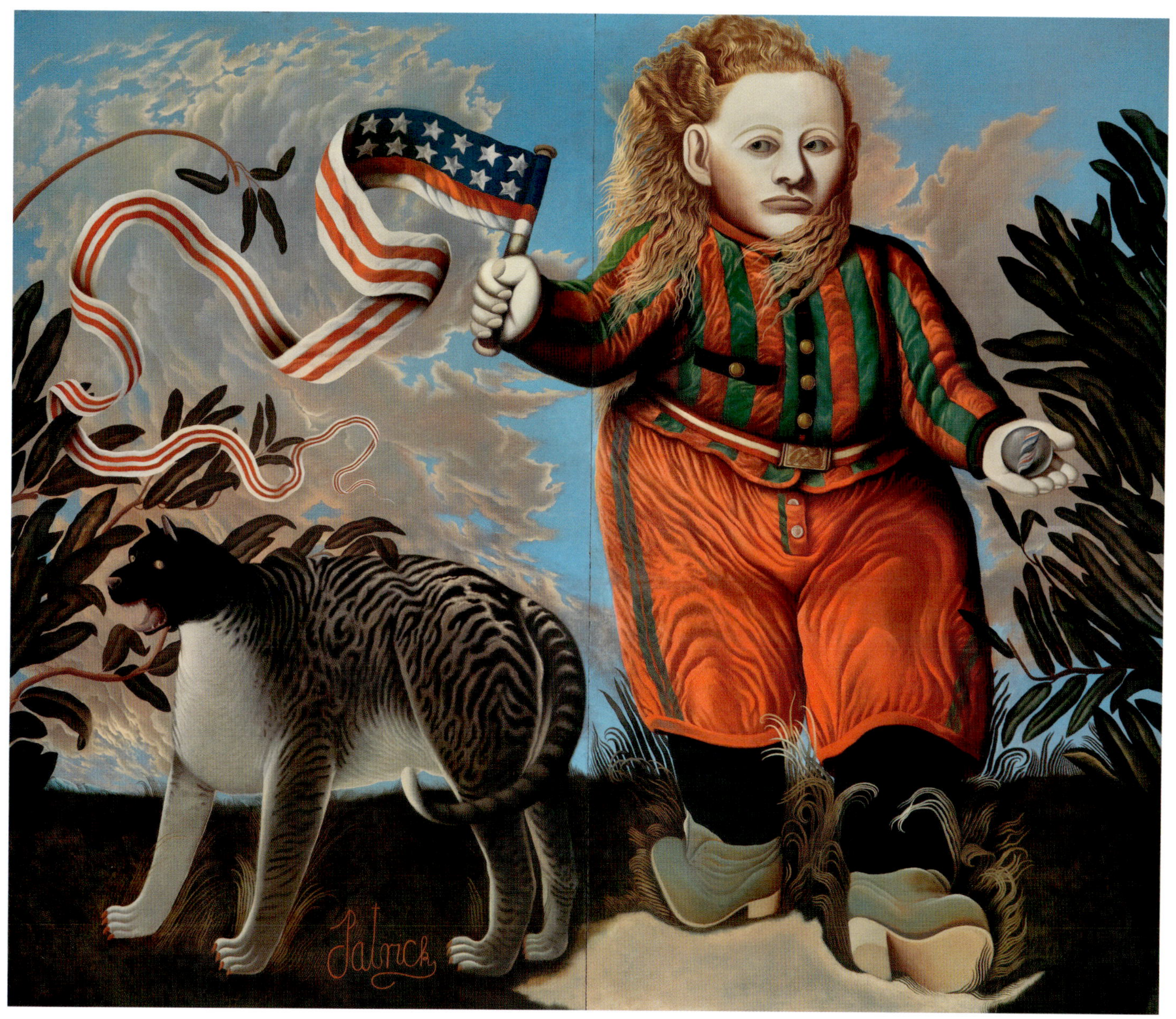

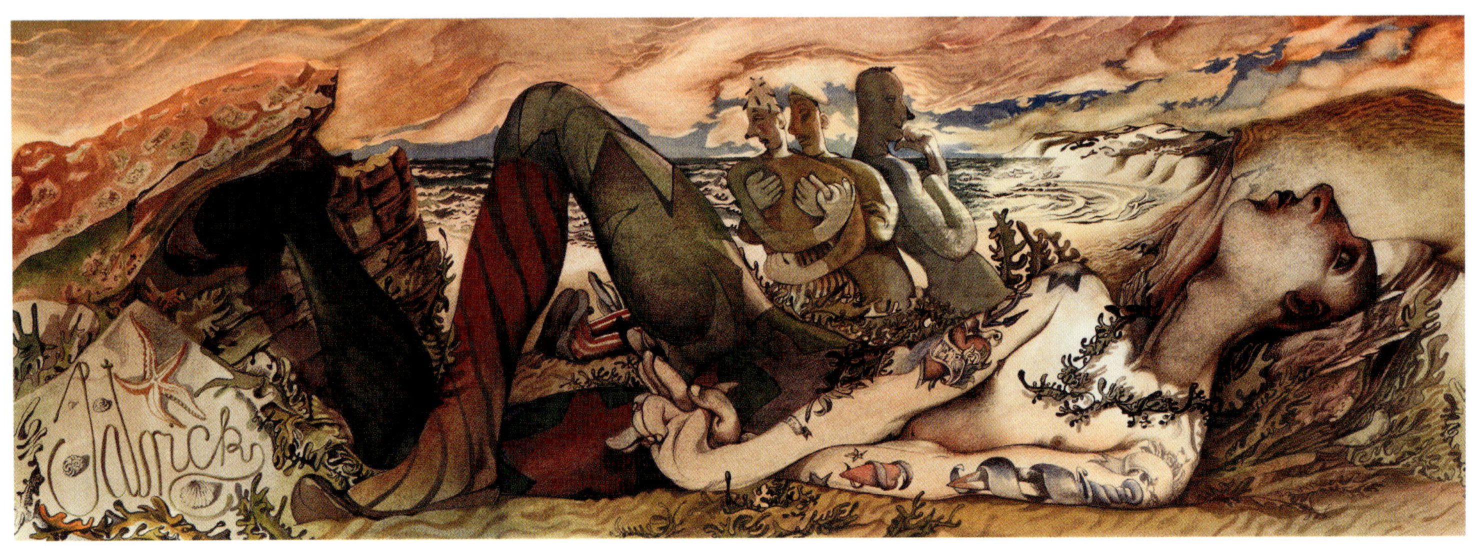

A Circus Rest by the Sea, 1991
Signed as Patrick
Watercolour, ink, paper
26.1cm × 71.7cm (unframed)
Bought by Glasgow Museums, 1995
PR.1995.8

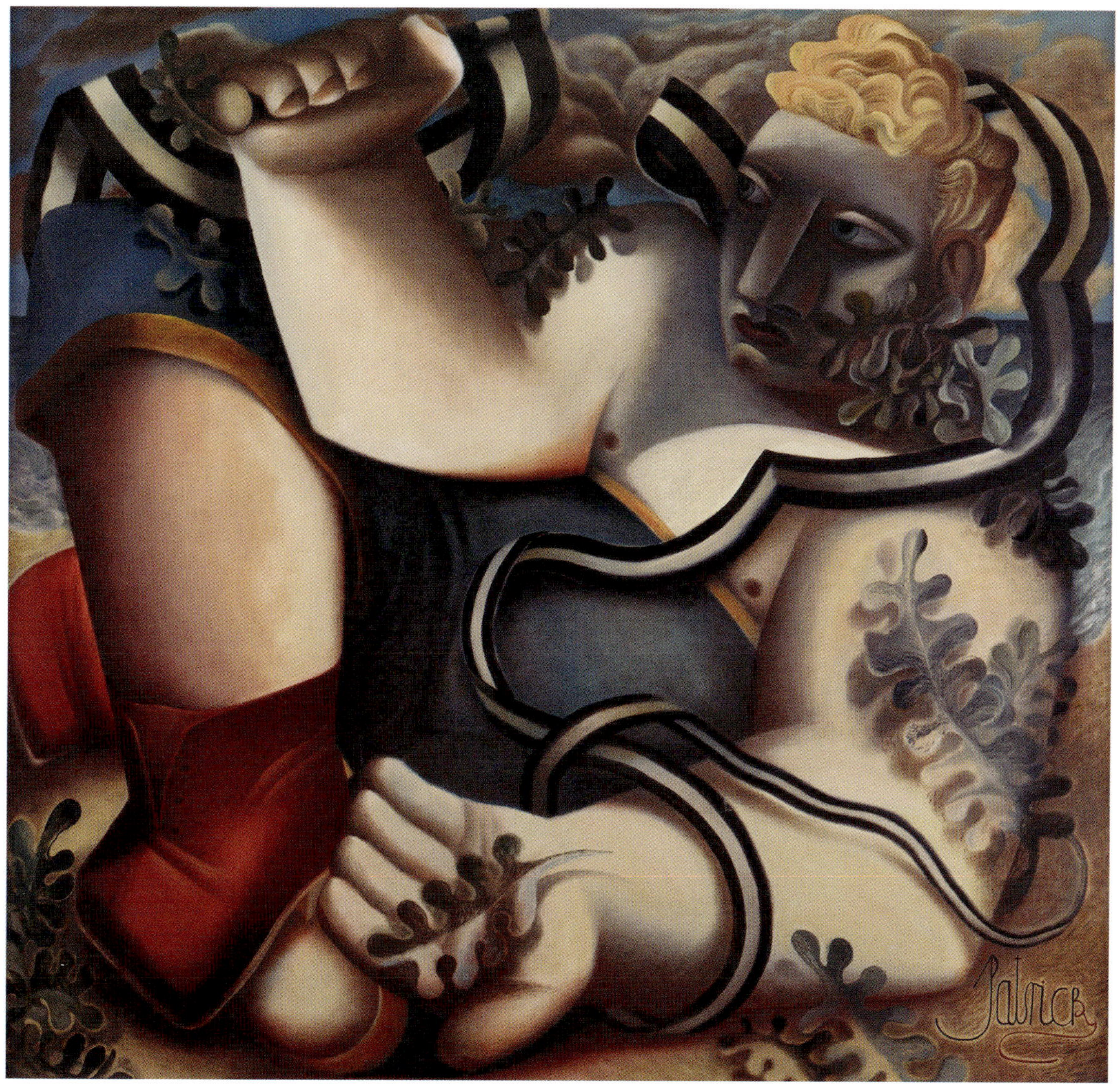

Dark Victory, 1995
Signed as Patrick
Oil on canvas
140cm × 146cm
Lent by Adriano
Martinelli

Although Byrne
moved away from
being Patrick in the
early 1970s, he does
sign work that way if
he feels it is a Patrick
work. This 1995
painting was used
for the cover of Gerry
Rafferty's 2003 album
Another World. The
signature 'Patrick' can
be seen at the bottom
right.

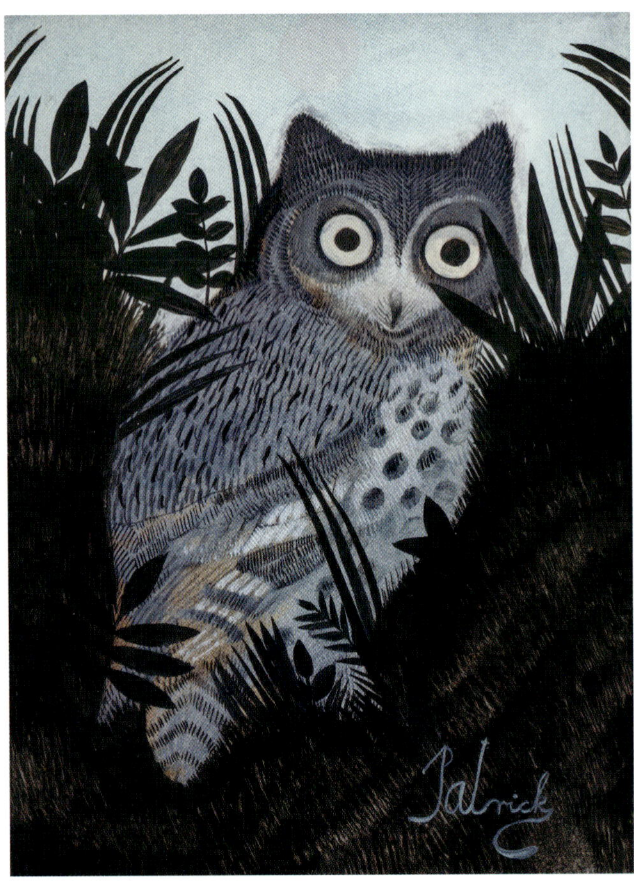

Owl, about 1968
Signed as Patrick
Watercolour, gouache, ink on paper
49cm × 40.5cm
Lent by Luca Martinelli

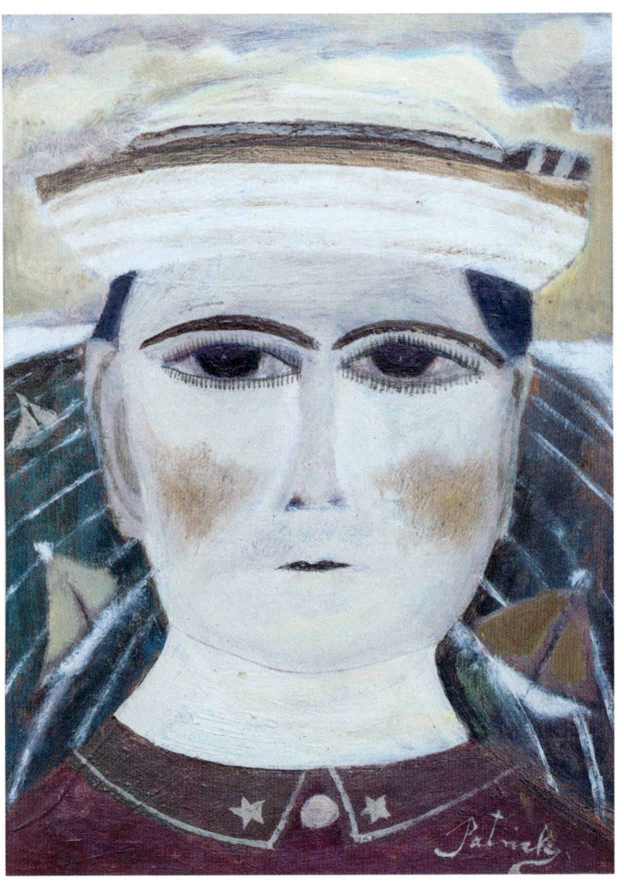

Jock, about 1967
Signed as Patrick
Oil on panel
47.5cm × 39.5cm
Lent by Adriano Martinelli

'Jock' is a Scottish shortening of the name John. Byrne gave this painting to Eric Lister, one of the Directors of the Portal Gallery, telling him it was of Byrne's son, also called John. 'Jock' appears in other Patrick paintings such as *Jock and the Tiger Cat* (see opposite), painted a year later, though it could be argued that there he represents Byrne rather than his son.

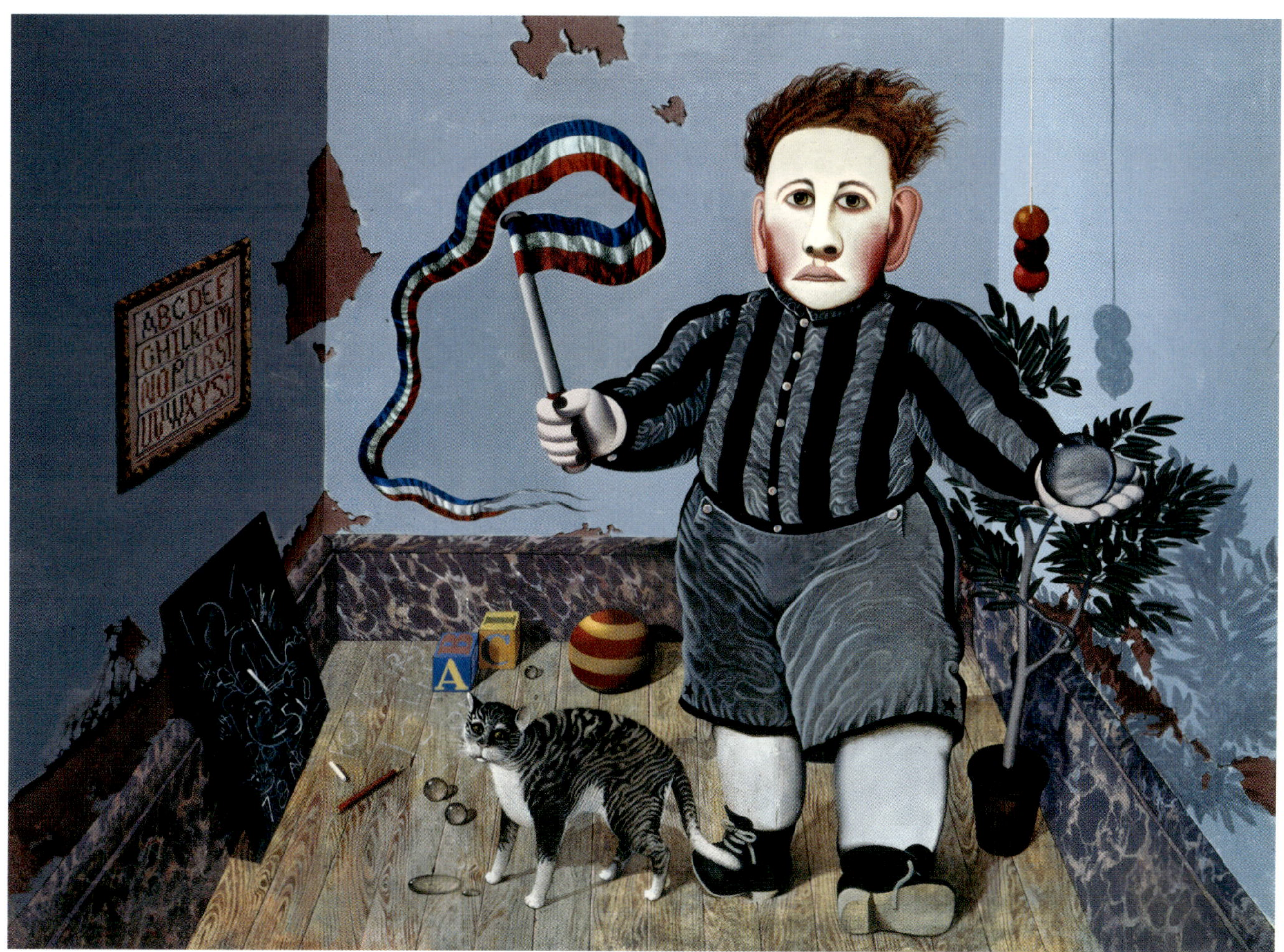

Jock and the Tiger Cat, 1968
Signed as Patrick
Oil on canvas, 88.3cm × 112.9cm
Courtesy of Perth Museum and
Art Gallery, Perth and Kinross
Council, Scotland

This painting is a great example of Byrne's skill at painting as Patrick. At first glance these works can look childlike or naive, but look closer and you see the skill in details such the wooden floor and the glass orb. The start of some signature elements in Byrne's work, such as scratchy graffiti or cats, can be seen too. The many elements from Byrne's childhood hint that the Jock in this painting is Byrne, rather than any other person, and it could be considered a self portrait. This work was commissioned by a Mrs Johnstone, whose name is drawn, as if in chalk, on the floor.

Murals

John Byrne has created three large-scale murals in his career, two in open-air locations in Glasgow and one in a theatre in Edinburgh. His background in design and creating theatre sets, mixed with his sheer artistic talent, made him the perfect choice for these huge projects.

Boy on Dogback – Glasgow's first gable-end mural

In 1974 the Scottish Arts Council, working with the Third Eye Centre (now the CCA) and its Director Tim McGrath, commissioned four gable-end murals in Glasgow. Byrne won the first commission bid and created a stunning gable-end mural in Crawford Street, Partick. The work was in the style of Patrick, and took two weeks to complete.

Local children graffitied the work, along the bottom edge. Byrne repeatedly painted over this, until one morning he found the statement 'Painter put your brush away, Tiny Partick are here to stay.' Byrne found this funny, so left it as part of the final work. The mural was embraced by local residents and admired for years, until the flats were eventually demolished, the mural surviving only in photographs.

Boy on Dog, Partick, 1975
Eric Watt
Colour slide
Glasgow Museums, Eric Watt
Collection
ME.2010.17.1852

The gable-end mural by John Byrne in Crawford St, Partick. Rubbish accumulated during the Glasgow Dust Cart Driver's Strike of 1975 is piled up in front.

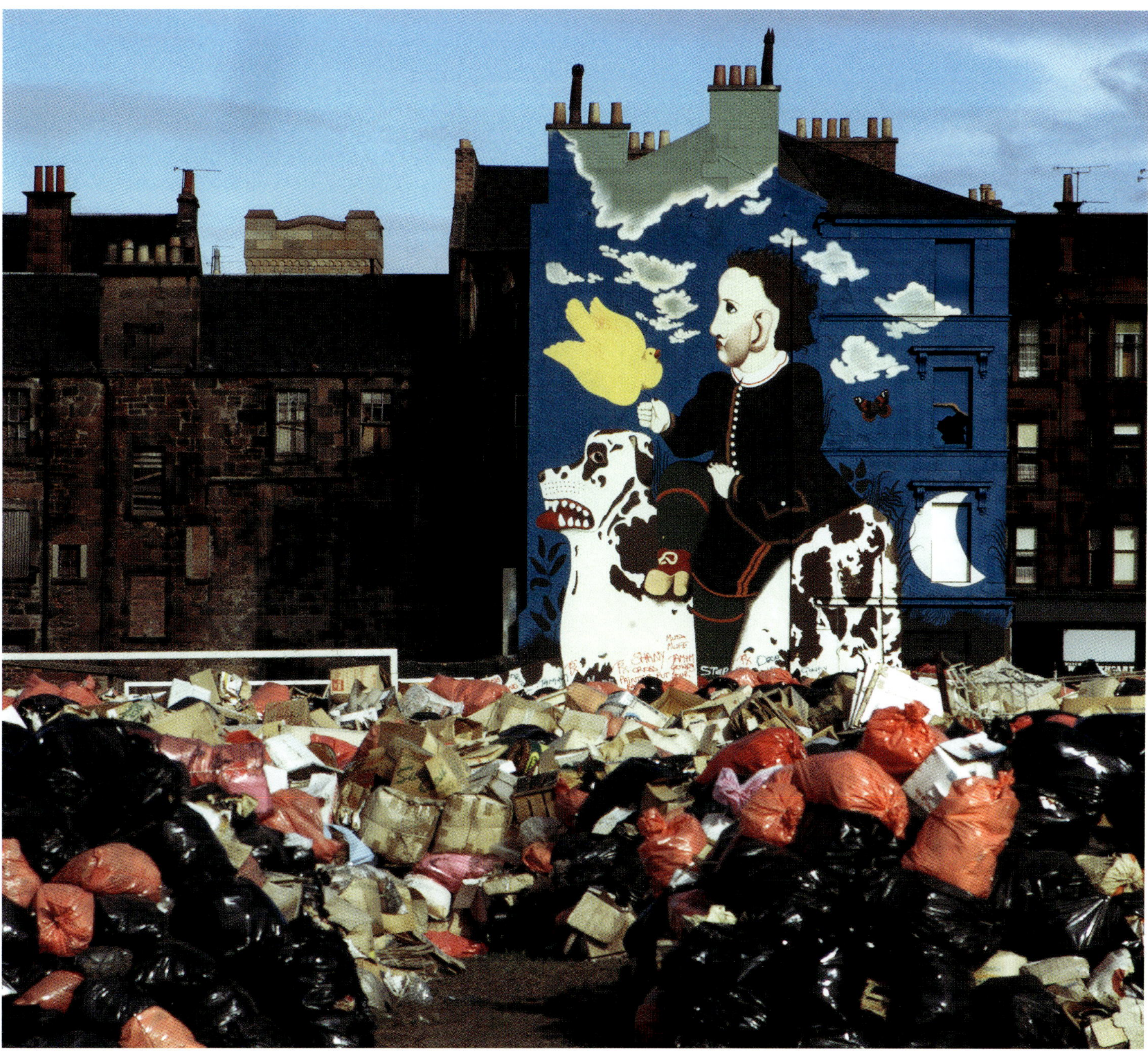

King's Theatre, Edinburgh

In 2013, Byrne was commissioned to paint a mural for the King's Theatre in Edinburgh. The mural sits on the dome above the audience as they wait for the curtain to go up. It is filled with theatrical references, and the two masks symbolizing comedy and tragedy are positioned over the stage. Shakespeare's famous line 'All the world's a stage', from *As You Like It*, wraps around them. The sun and the moon are chased round the dome by the night sky as a flowing female muse, and a figure in a diamond-patterned leotard. The harlequin is a character Byrne explores in other works (see p. 89). The mural depicts storytelling as timeless, never ending.

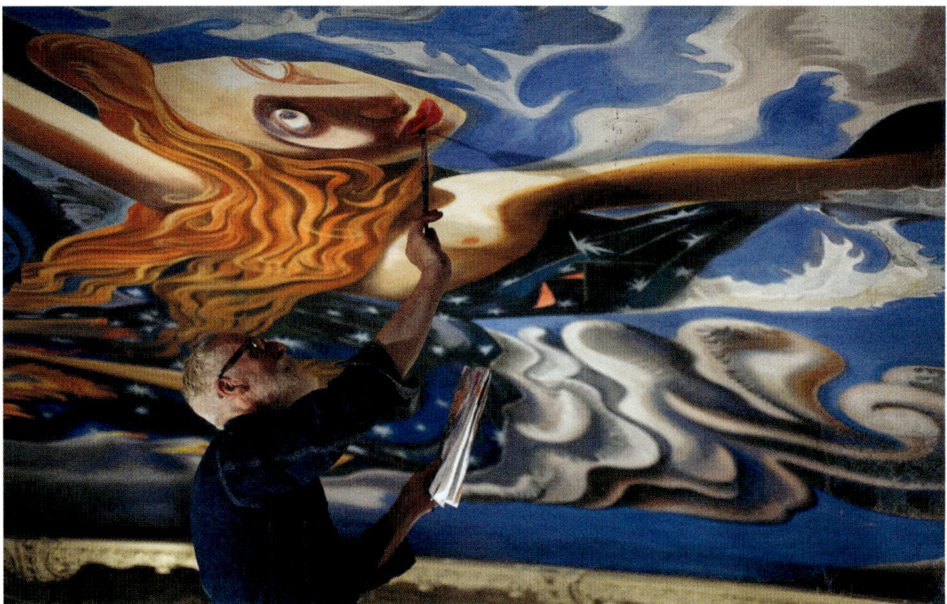

This photograph, taken by Ron O'Donnell, shows Byrne at work on the mural.

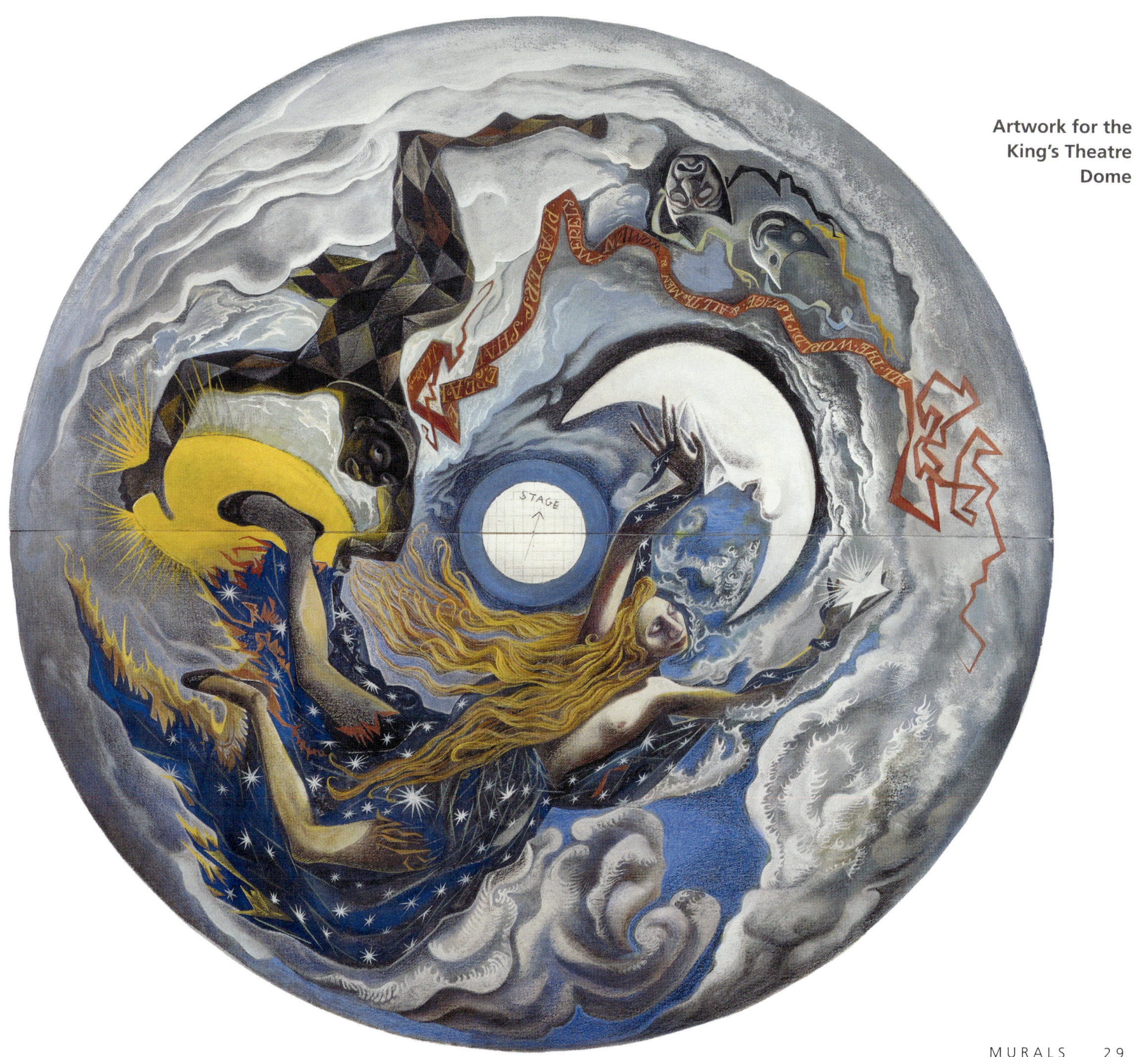

Artwork for the King's Theatre Dome

Billy Connolly

In 2017, to celebrate Scottish comedian Billy Connolly's seventy-fifth birthday, the BBC commissioned three portraits of Connolly for the programme *Billy Connolly: Portrait of a Lifetime*. These were then reproduced as murals around Glasgow.

Byrne was one of those asked to paint a portrait. This was fitting, as not only has Byrne known Connolly for years, but he also created the first ever gable-end mural for the city, *Boy on Dogback*.

The other two portraits were created by artists Jack Vettriano and Rachel Maclean. All three portraits were then turned into murals by artists Rogue-one and Art Pistol.

John Byrne is a genius, and an astounding artist and playwright. I love him.
Billy Connolly, from *Windswept and Interesting, My Autobiography* (John Murray Press, 2021)

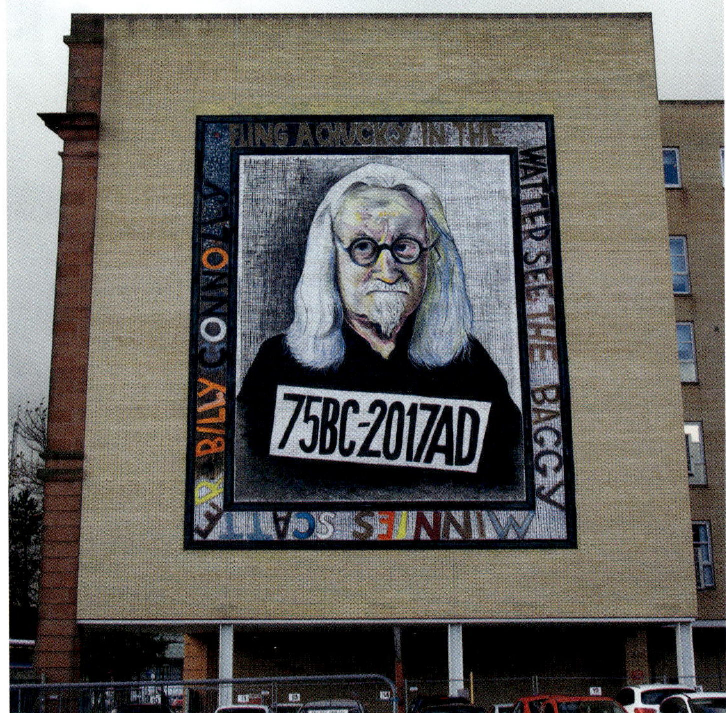

opposite: The artwork for the mural.

left: The mural in situ in Glasgow.

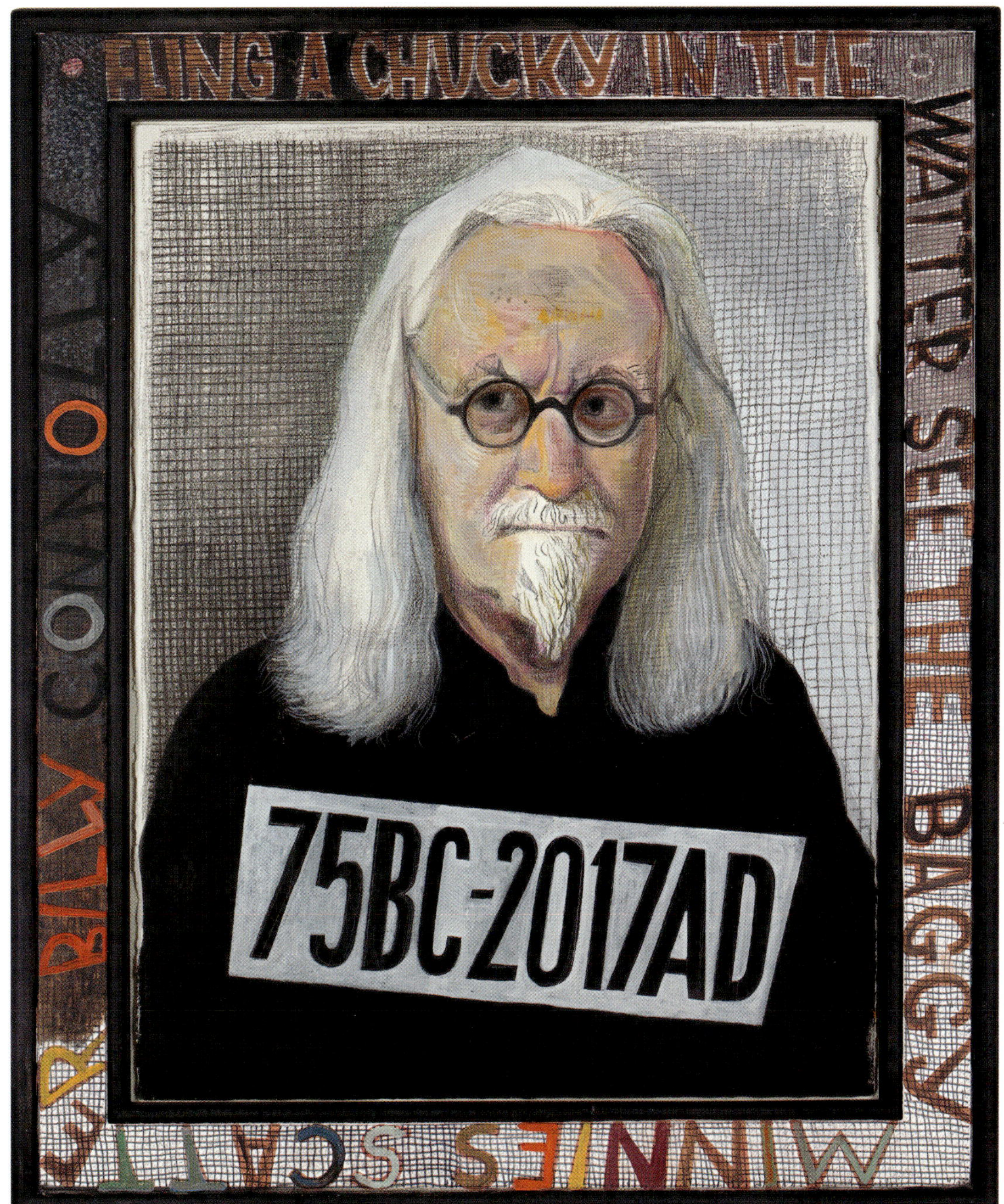

FLING A CHUCKY IN THE
WATTER SEE THE BAGGY
MINNIES SCATTER
BILLY CONNOLLY
75BC-2017AD

Music and influences

Music has been a big influence in Byrne's life. As a young boy and teenager living in Paisley, he loved the 'new' American music, especially rhythm and blues, and rock 'n' roll. This features heavily in his writing, particularly the BBC productions *Tutti Frutti* and *Your Cheatin' Heart*. In his play *The Slab Boys,* the nods to American pop culture can be seen in the poster of James Dean, and the female lead Lucille, the name BB King gave to all his guitars.

Byrne's artwork is in millions of homes around the world, on album covers for musicians such as The Beatles, Donovan, The New Humble Bums, Gerry Rafferty, and Stealers Wheel.

From his Patrick era onwards, Byrne has painted black musicians, always from a position of respect and celebration. Brought up in Paisley, a weaving town with links to the cotton trade, he was aware that there was much more to black history than the music he loved. Time in Los Angeles, animating songs by the singer Donovan, brought home the reality of this, tarnishing the sheen of 'the American Dream'.

Cantina Chimichangas, 2006
Ink on scraper board
41cm × 49.5cm
Lent by Adriano Martinelli

This fun drawing shows Byrne's skill and graphic influence. The two skeletons could be Byrne, with his signature cigarette and his favourite hat at the time, and Gerry Rafferty, sitting with his guitar.

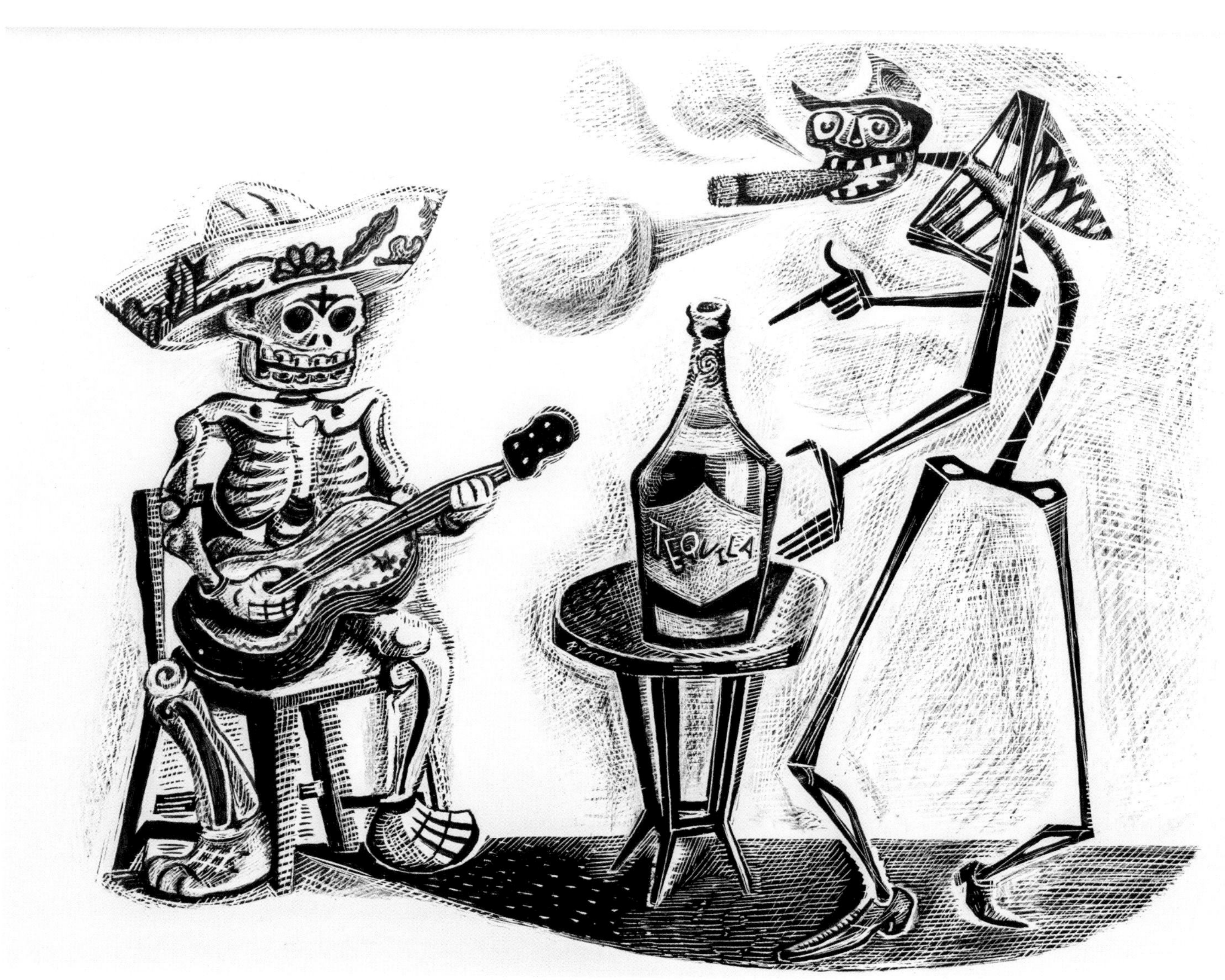
TEQUILA

Incident, Underwood Lane,
about 2011
Oil on board, signature in pastel
118cm × 95cm
Lent by Adriano Martinelli

Named after the Paisley street
where Gerry Rafferty was born,
Underwood Lane is Byrne's latest
play. It has an eclectic 'jukebox'
feel, much like his classic TV series
Tutti Frutti. Delayed due to the
pandemic, the play opens in the
summer of 2022.

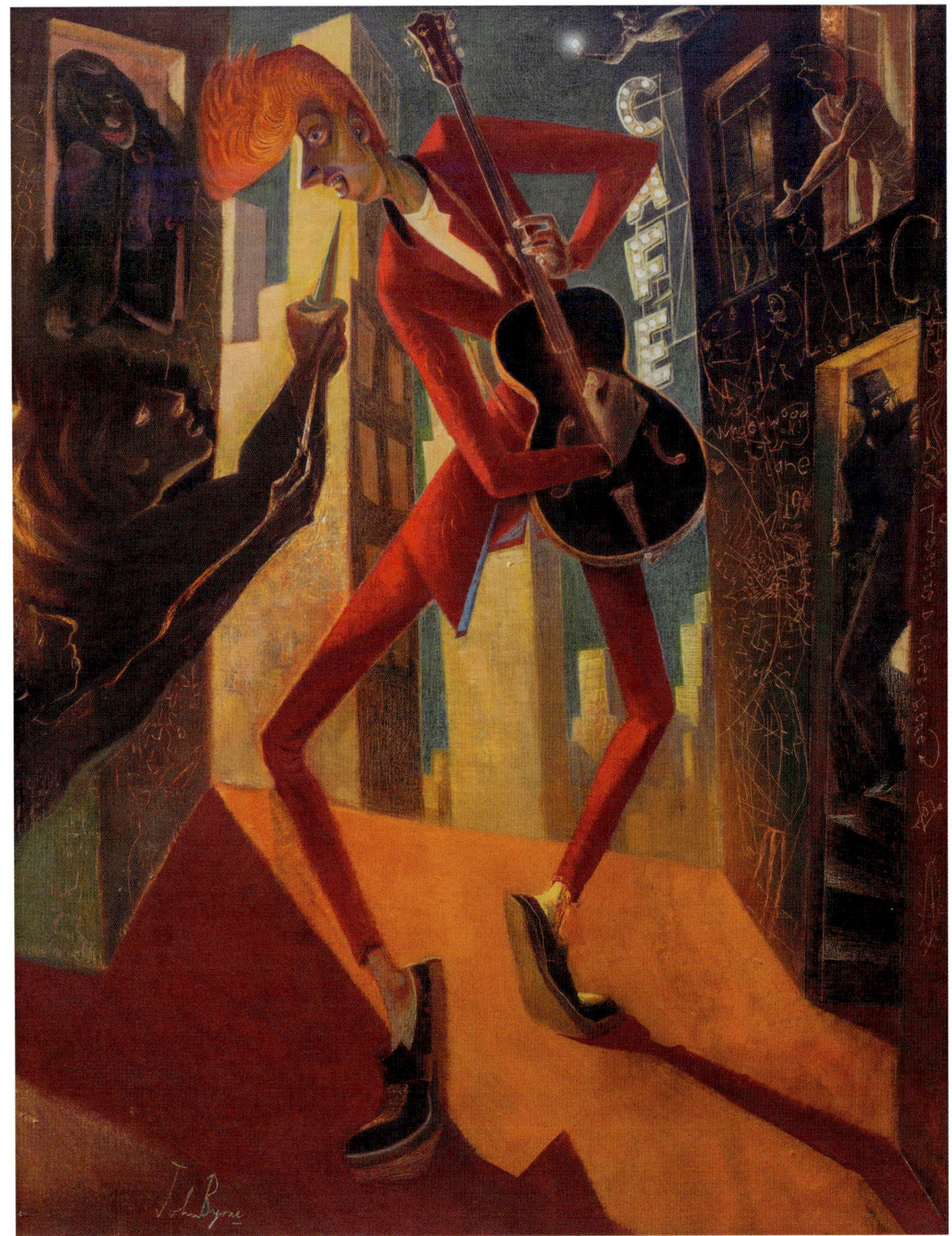

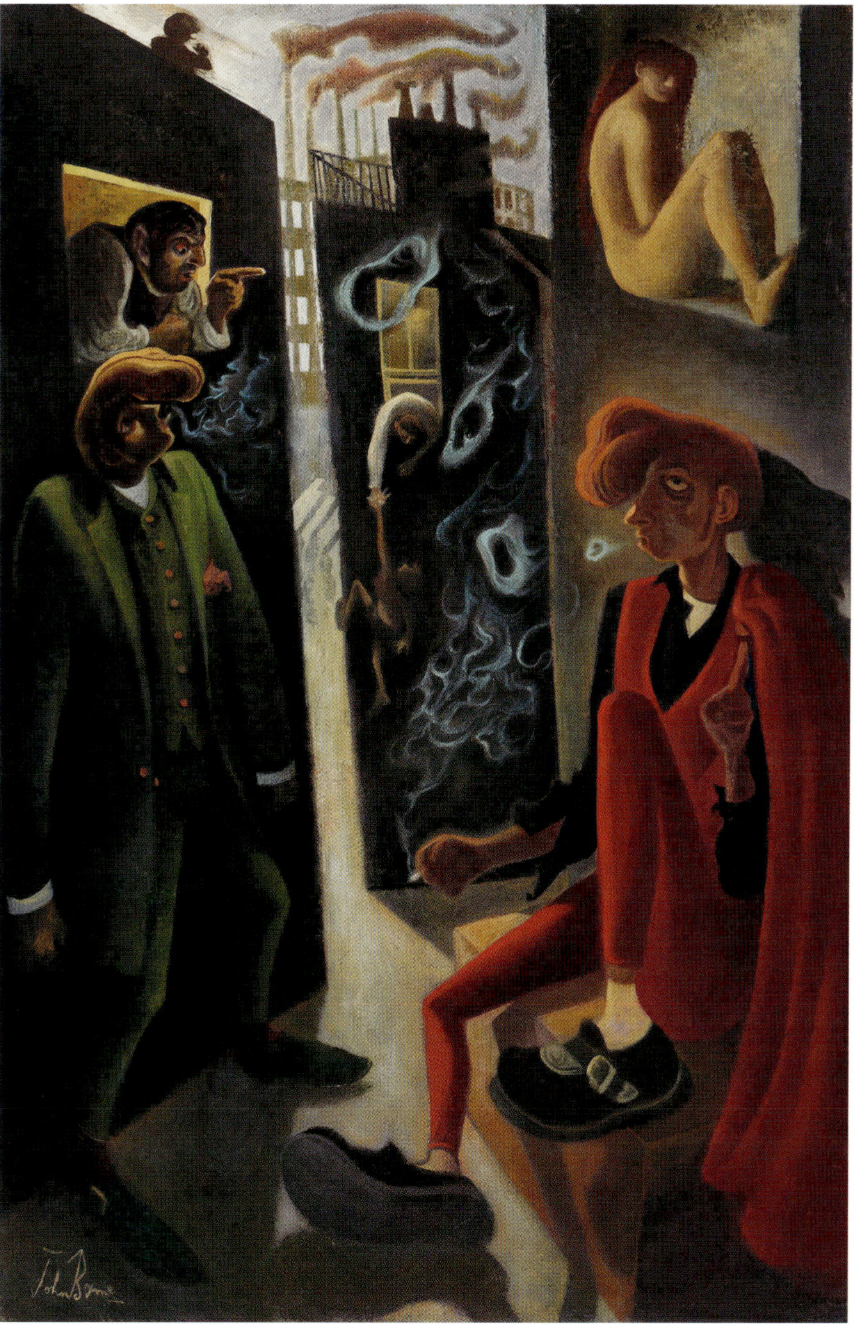

O My Love, 2014
Oil on Formica board
59cm × 52cm
Private Collection

Another scene from Byrne's *Underwood Lane* series. The street is the same but the characters are in different positions, suggesting time has passed.

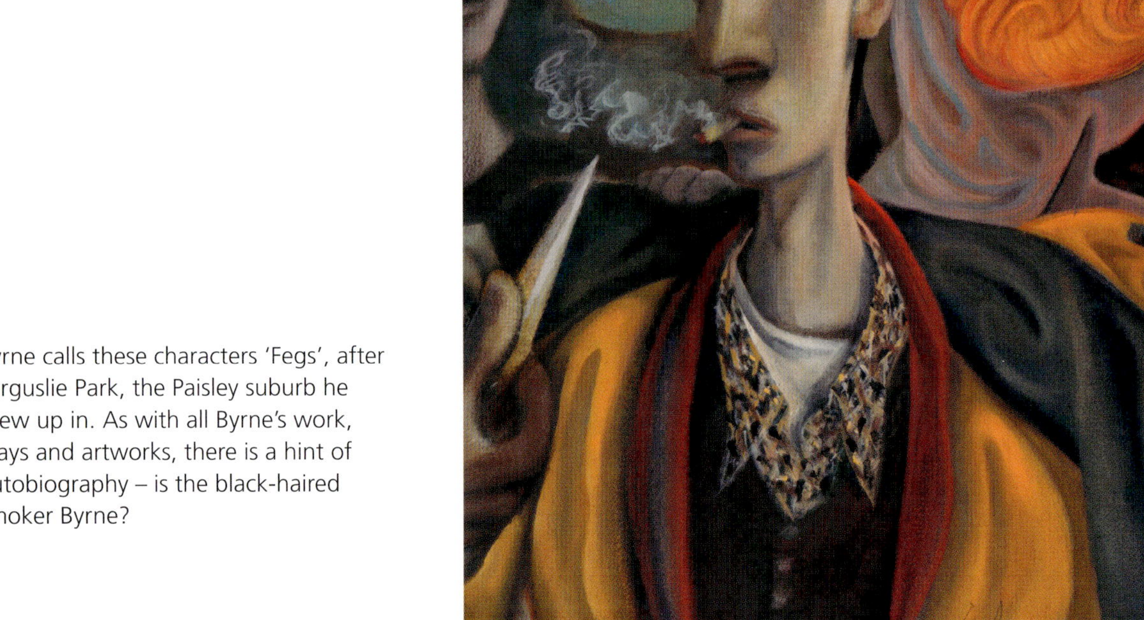

Byrne calls these characters 'Fegs', after
Ferguslie Park, the Paisley suburb he
grew up in. As with all Byrne's work,
plays and artworks, there is a hint of
autobiography – is the black-haired
smoker Byrne?

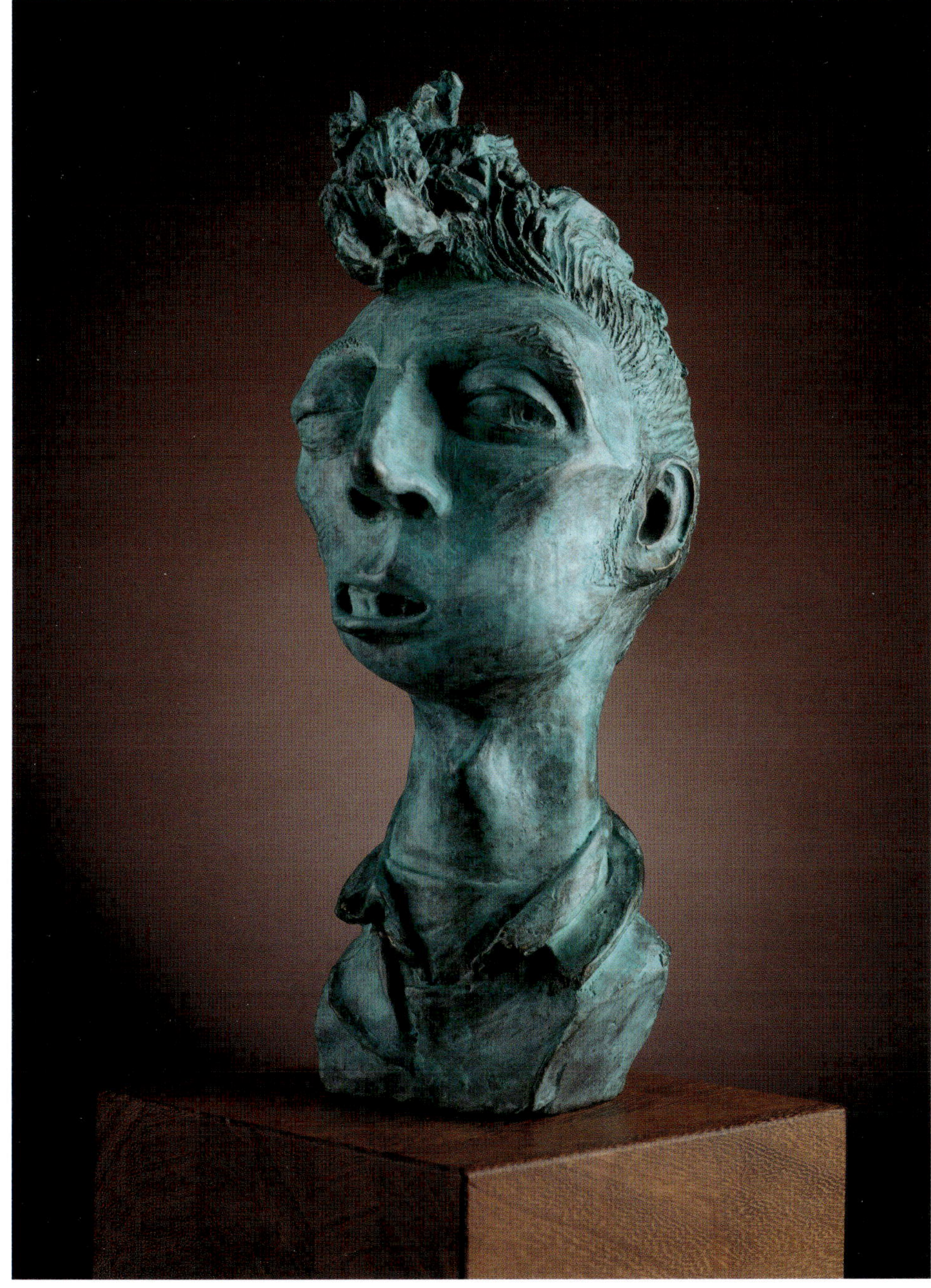

A Feg, 2009
Bronze on wood base
45cm × 16cm × 16cm
Private Collection

Inspired by pottery classes he and Jeanine
took at the Salisbury Centre, Edinburgh,
Byrne made this bust.

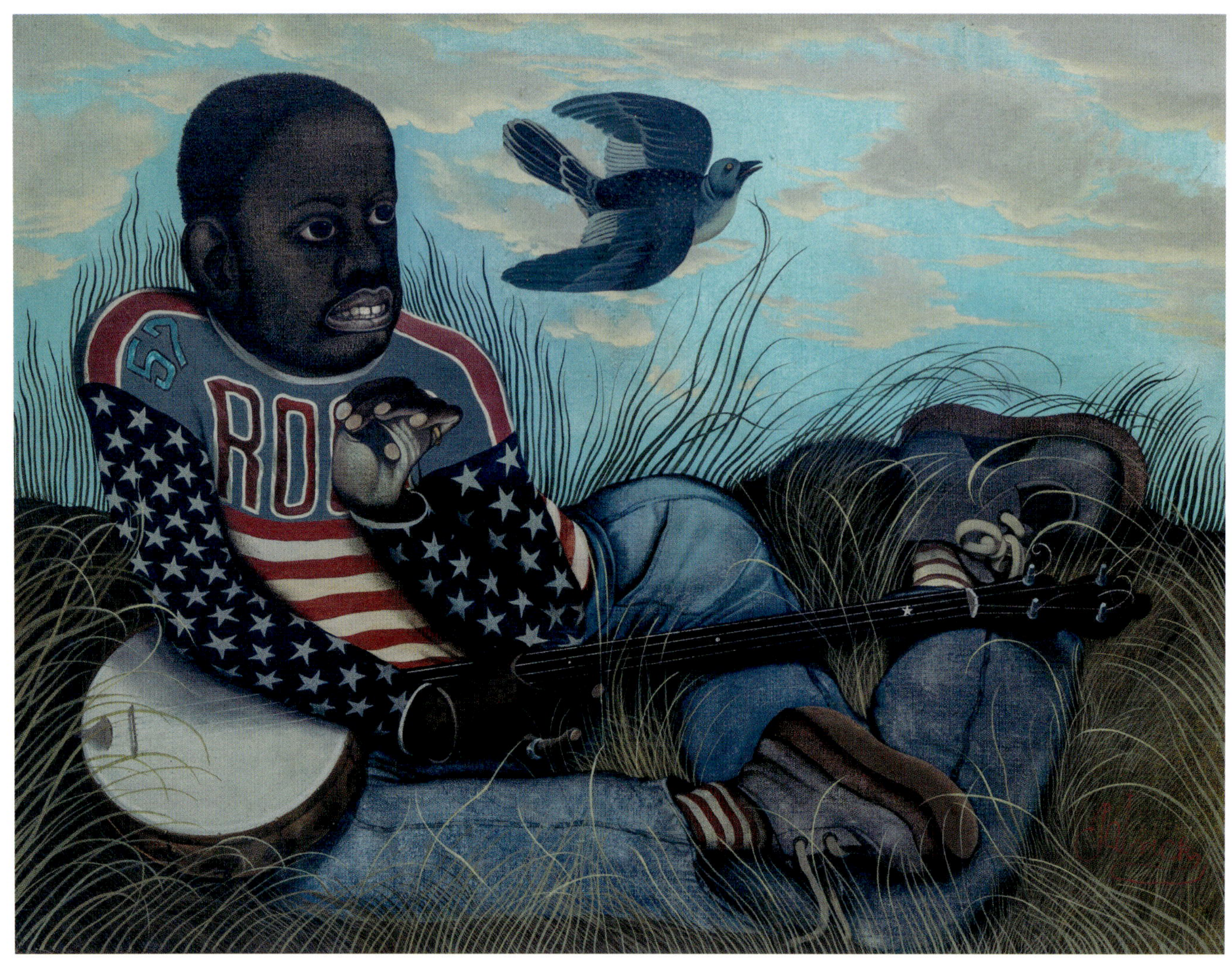

American Boy with Banjo, 1967–68
Signed Patrick
Oil on canvas, 63cm × 73cm
Lent by Adriano Martinelli

This was painted as Patrick, and before Byrne visited America. He particularly enjoys depicting musicians. Like many young people at that time, he was highly influenced by rock 'n' roll and blues, and the black culture they were rooted in.

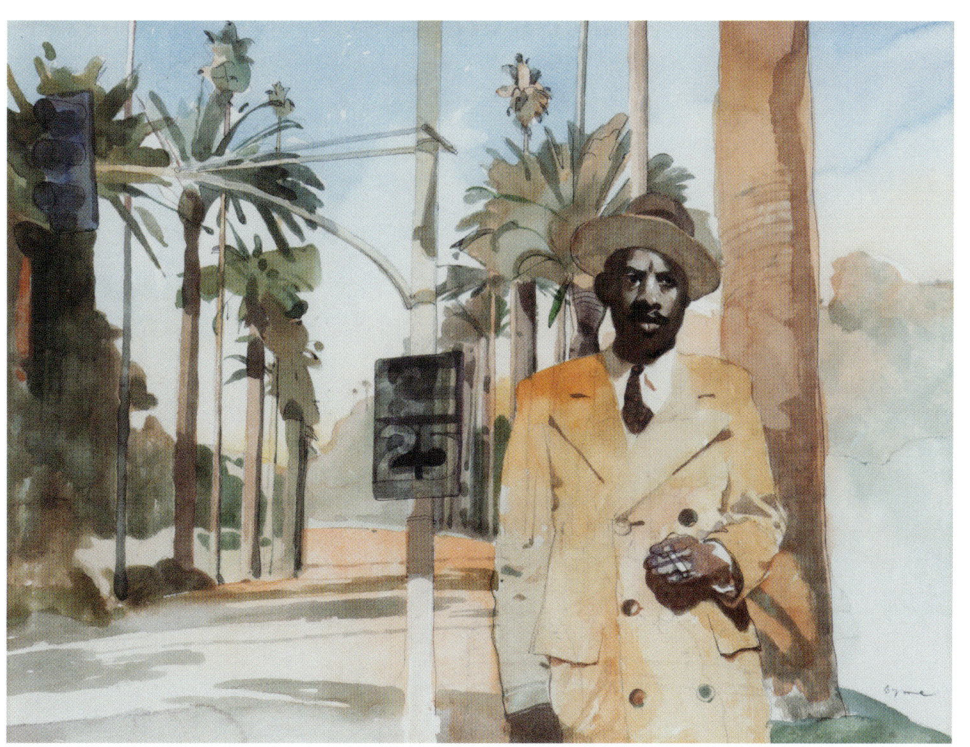

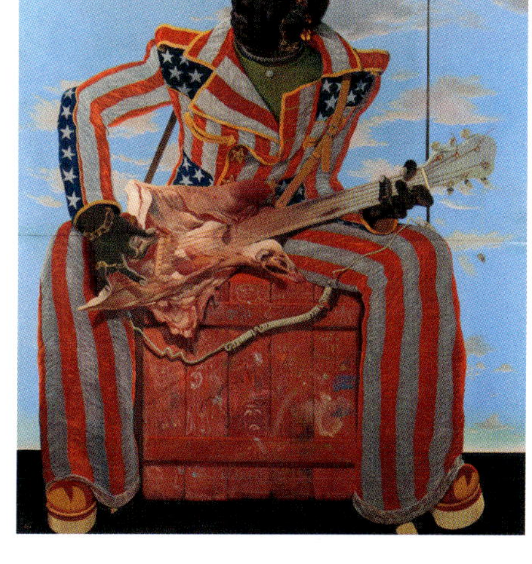

Burnt Orange LA, 1971
Watercolour on paper
38.7cm × 55.8cm
Lent by Martha Rafferty

This is from a series of watercolour studies painted when Byrne was in Los Angeles working with the singer Donovan. Byrne loved American R&B music and often included people of colour in his work. The influence of Los Angeles is evident in the large-scale paintings of black guitar players from his Third Eye Centre exhibition. These included *National Velvet* (pictured right), in which the guitar is a flayed American eagle, showing Byrne's understanding of racism in America towards people of colour.

National Velvet, 1975
Oil on plywood
214cm × 202cm
Renfrewshire Museums Collection

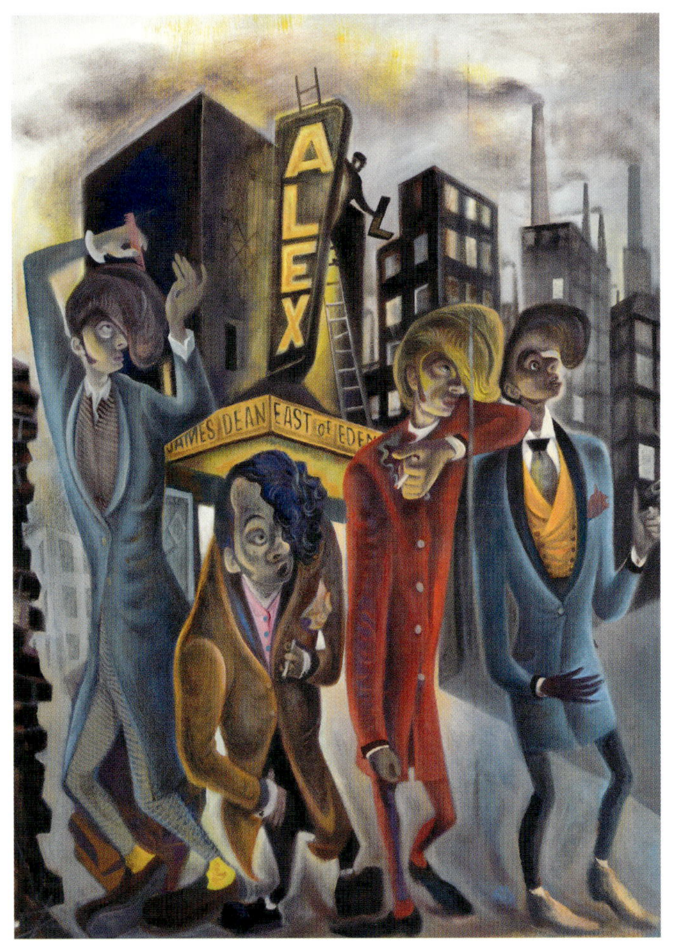

ALEX
JAMES DEAN EAST of EDEN

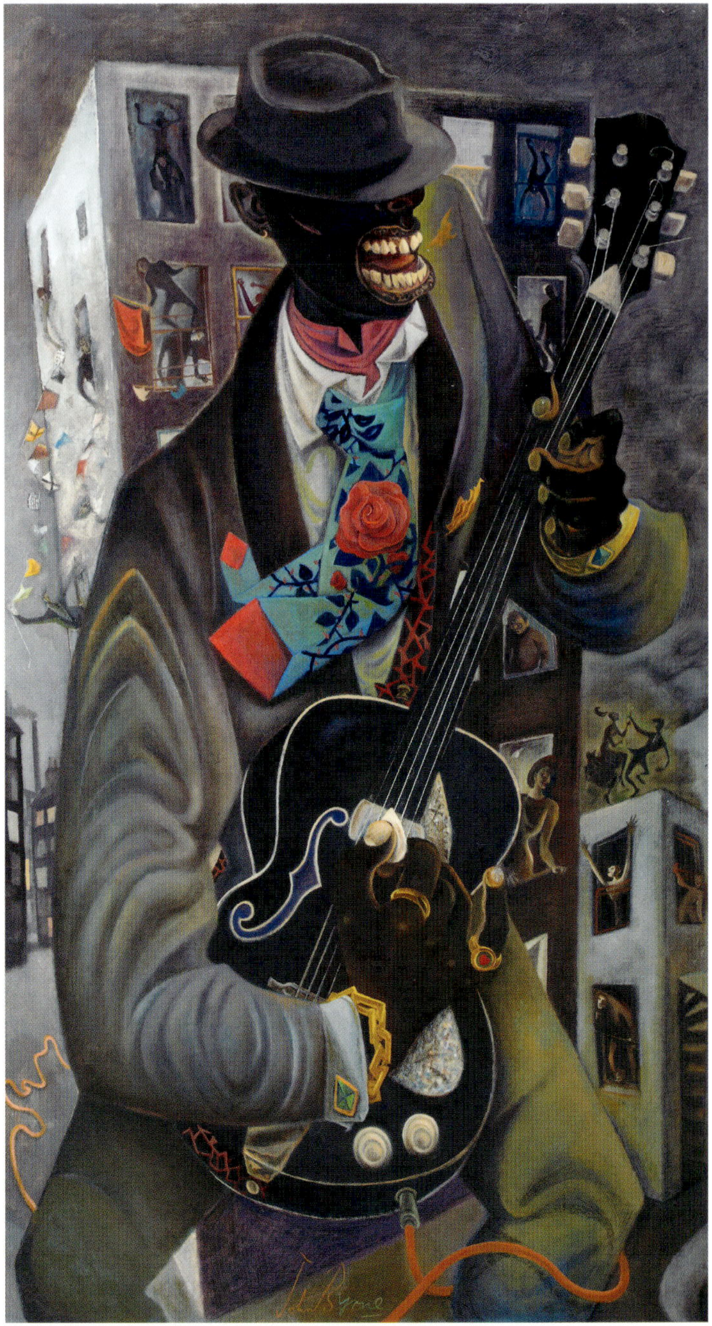

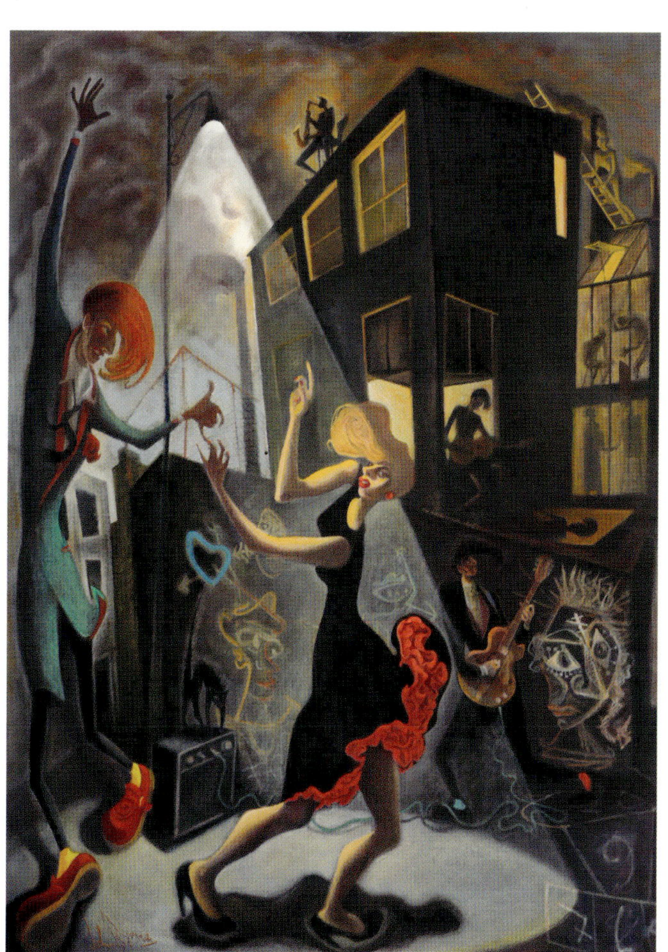

The Messiah (triptych), 2015
Central image: oil on board
157cm × 85.5cm
Left and right images: oil on paper, conté pastel and chalk
Each 110cm × 79.5cm
Lent by Adriano Martinelli

In this work Byrne said he wanted to depict the leader of a fictional city. It blends the subject and tone of his Paisley *Underwood Lane* works with the neon and skyscrapers of American cities, perhaps harking back to Byrne's childhood dreams and influences.

Billy Connolly and Banjo, diptych, about 1974
Oil on panel
244.1cm × 122.1cm (each panel, unframed)
Given to Glasgow Museums by the artist, 1977; *Banjo* given in 2017
PP.1977.26 and PP.2017.18

This diptych of Billy Connolly featured in Byrne's Third Eye Centre, Glasgow, exhibition which opened on 19 June 1975. For years Glasgow Museums owned this painting of Connolly, unaware it had a second section until Byrne saw the work on a visit. Byrne kindly re-painted the missing panel and donated it to Glasgow Museums in 2017.

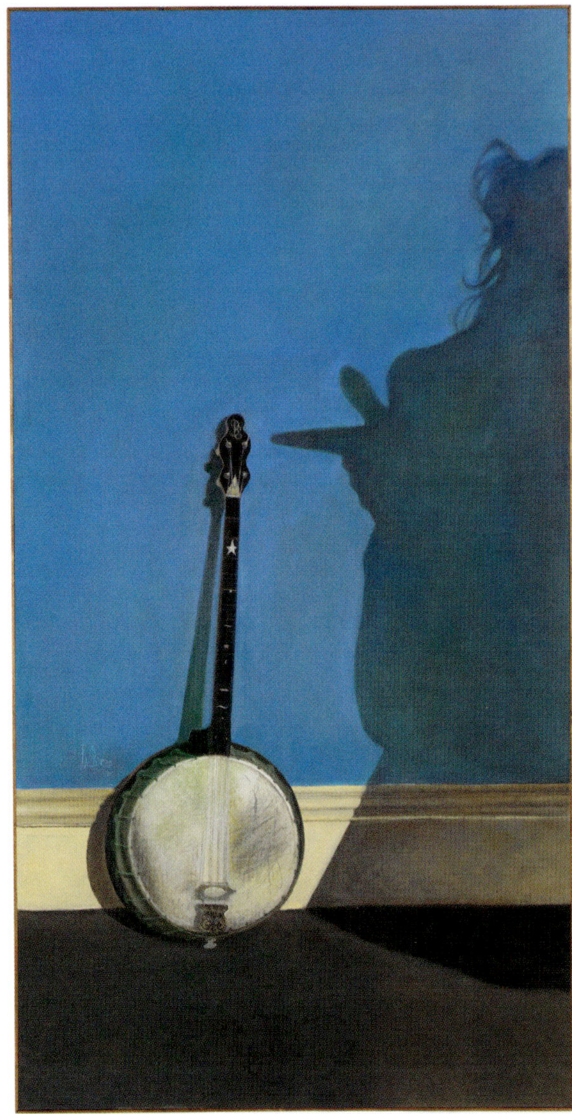

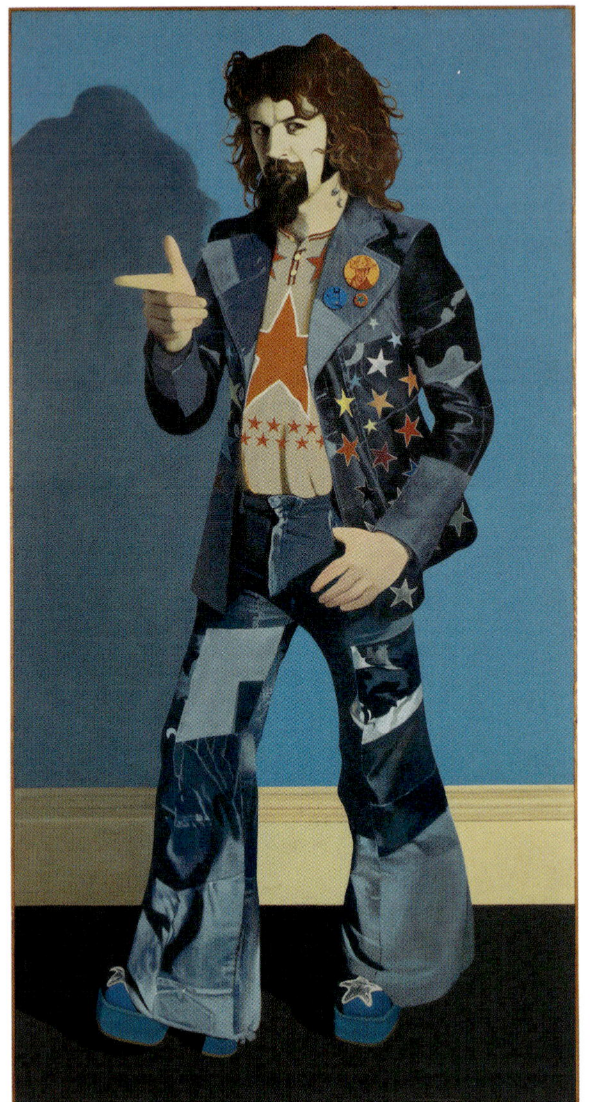

Portrait of Gerry Rafferty, painted guitar,
about 1970
Martin D-35 acoustic guitar, paint
103.5cm × 39.6cm × 13cm
Lent by Martha Rafferty

Gerry Rafferty's iconic guitar was painted in
Byrne's Patrick era. Byrne painted covers for
Rafferty's albums, both solo and those with
the New Humble Bums and Stealers Wheel,
incorporating names and titles within the
picture, such as the tree spelling 'Gerry' and
the dog lead 'Rafferty'. Rafferty's song 'Patrick'
is about Byrne.

Child with Puppet, painted banjo, 1969
Signed Patrick
Animal skin, wood, string, painted surface
98cm × 28cm
Lent by Mr Benny Higgins and Mrs Sharon Higgins

This early example of Byrne
painting on musical
instruments features
classic Patrick
iconography
such as a child,
a flag and
glass orb.

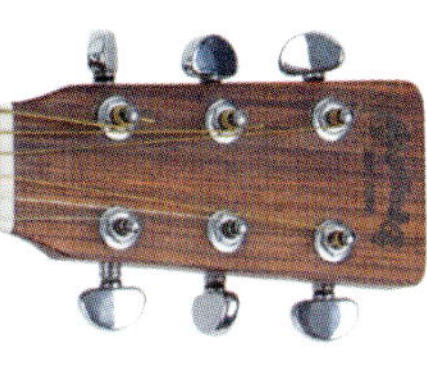

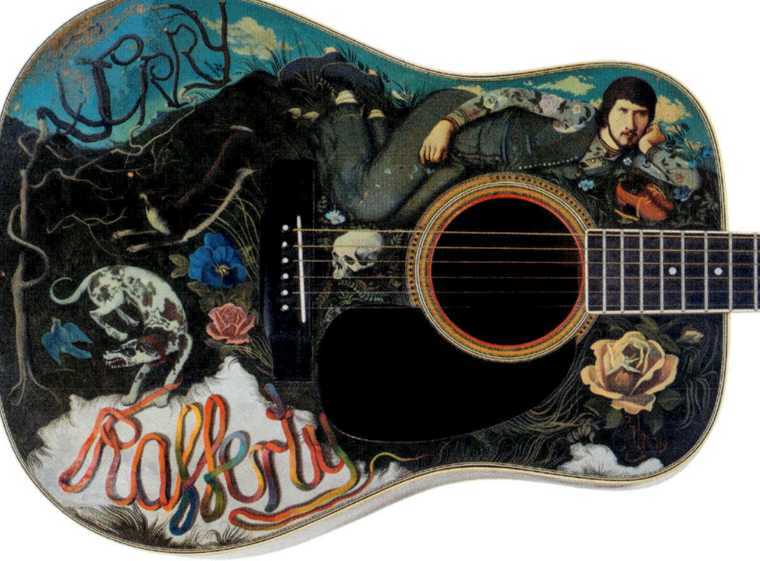

Writing

TV and Stage

At art school, Byrne would write to his fellow students and friends as the fictional character Francis Seneca McDade from Shoogley Peg. McDade became the focus of his first play *Writer's Cramp* (1976), and this parallel production of writing and art continued through his career.

Byrne contends that his slow typing process, using one finger from each hand, allows him to think about what he is writing. Part of his process is physically drawing the characters, allowing them to take form so they can speak for themselves.

This process has helped him write plays such as *Writer's Cramp, Colquhoun and MacBryde* (1992), *The Slab Boys* series (1978), and *Underwood Lane* (2022). Byrne also wrote two BBC TV shows, *Tutti Frutti* and *Your Cheatin' Heart*.

He has designed sets for his own plays as well as iconic shows such as Billy Connolly's *The Great Northern Welly Boot Show* (1972), costumes for Scottish Opera and the Scottish National Theatre, and produced posters for numerous shows.

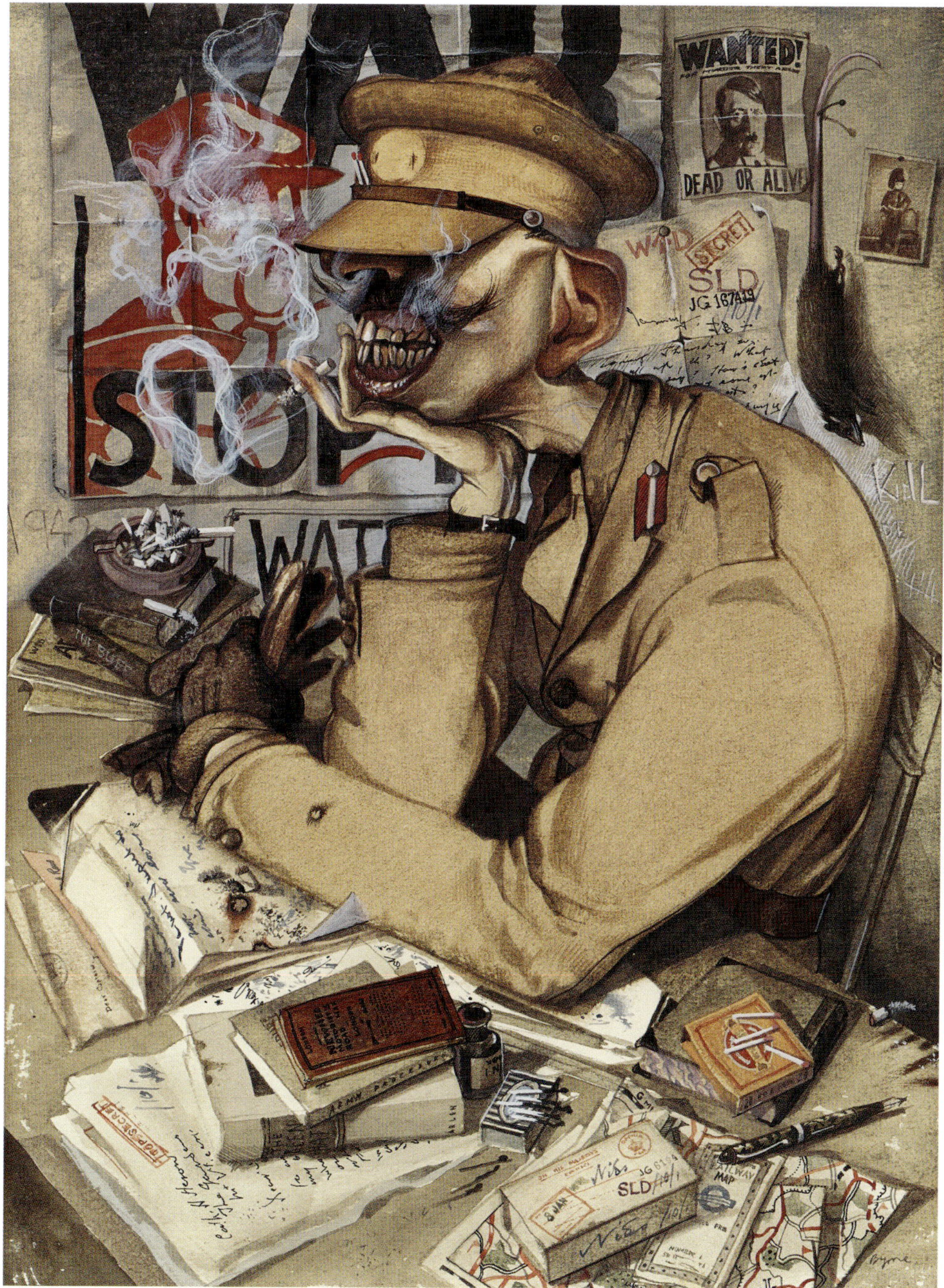

Writer's Cramp, 1975
Watercolour and body colour with ink
34cm × 24.13cm
From the private collection of Mr and
Mrs S Johnston

This piece was painted in 1975, helping
Byrne visualize and develop the play
Writer's Cramp. Two years later it
debuted at the Edinburgh Fringe to
critical acclaim.

The Slab Boys

The Slab Boys, as with all Byrne's work, is semi-autobiographical. Byrne was himself a 'slab boy' at AF Stoddard & Co. carpet factory, grinding paint for the carpet designers with a couple of other boys, one of whom was John Rafferty, musician Gerry Rafferty's older brother. The play revolves around three slab boys, Phil, Spanky and Hector, and all the action takes place in a carpet factory on a Friday in the winter of 1957, before a staff dance that evening.

Although the character of Phil McCann has the most similar journey to Byrne – in the play he is waiting to hear if he has a place at art school – each of the slab boys has a bit of Byrne in them, even the shy and timid Hector.

This seminal play, along with the three others (*Cuttin' a Rug*, *Still Life*, and *Nova Scotia*) which make up *The Slab Boys* 'trilogy' (it is very Byrne to refuse to stick to the definition of a trilogy as three!) are consistently part of the school curriculum. Repeatedly restaged, they are loved by successive generations, often providing pivotal roles in many young actors' careers.

The Slab Boys has been performed around the globe, but arguably its most stars-in-the-making-studded run was its 1983 New York debut, which included notable performances by then-unknowns Kevin Bacon, Sean Penn and Val Kilmer, together with Jackie Earle Haley, Brian Benben and Madeleine Potter.

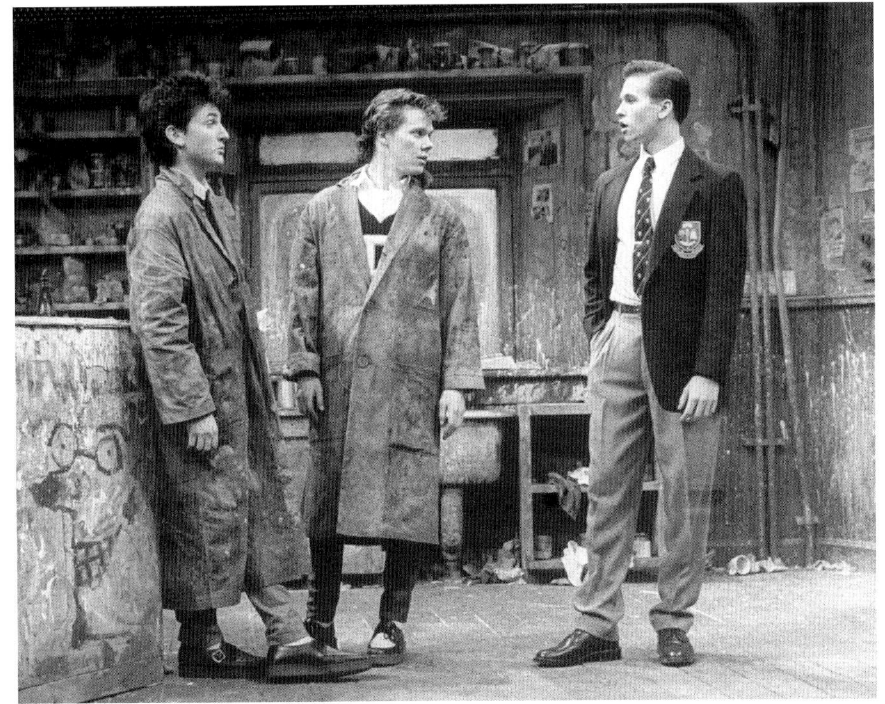

From left to right: Sean Penn, Kevin Bacon and Val Kilmer in a scene from the off-Broadway production of the play *The Slab Boys*.

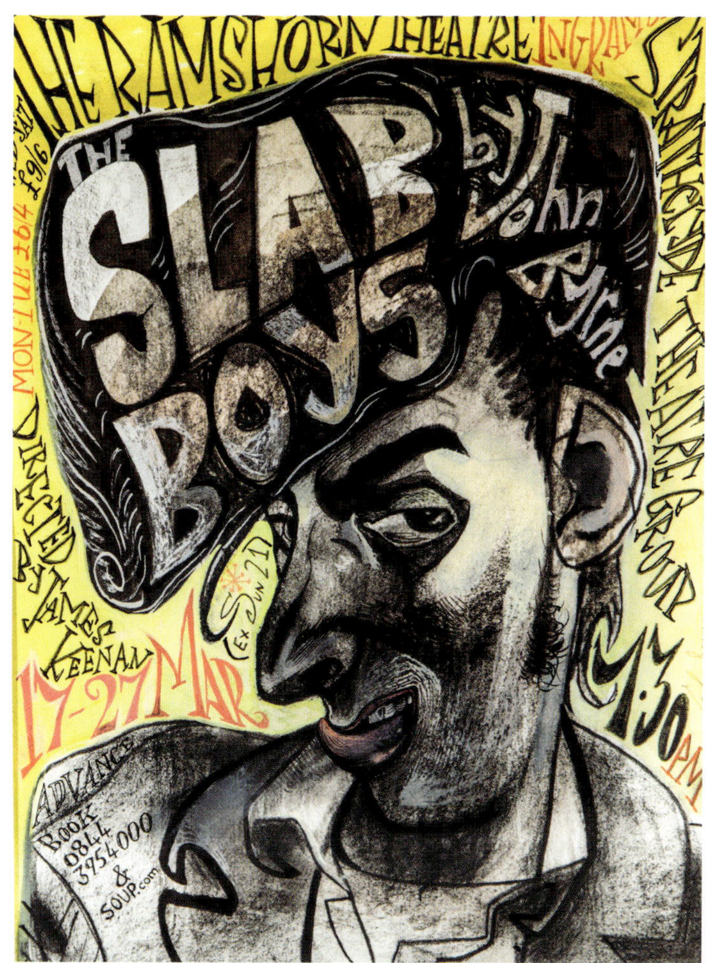

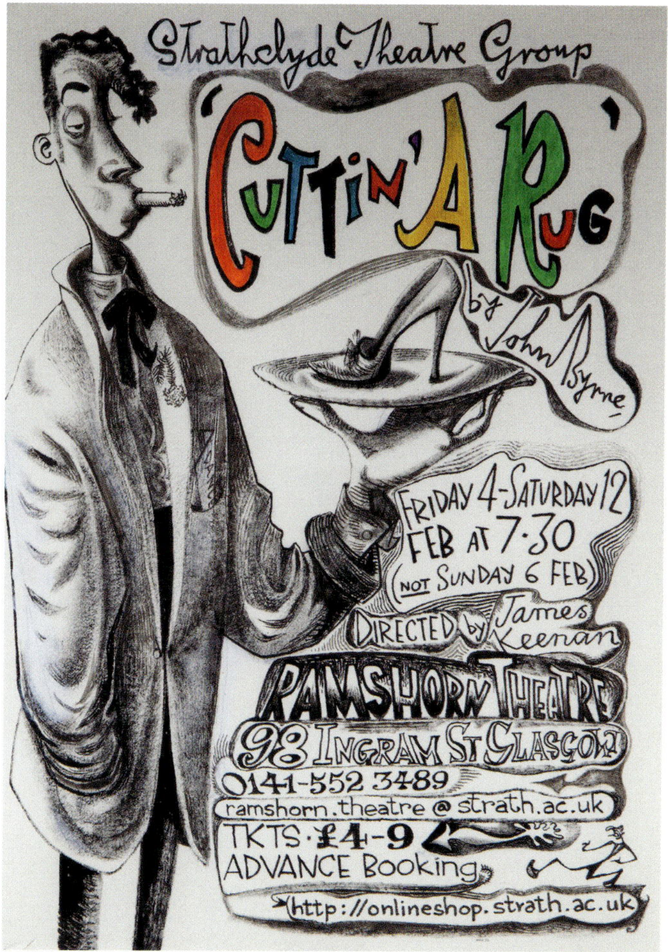

The Slab Boys, original poster artwork for the Ramshorn Theatre, 2009
Watercolour, ink and graphite on paper
57cm × 46cm
Private Collection, Charles Marks

Cuttin' A Rug, original poster artwork for the Ramshorn Theatre, 2011
Watercolour and ink on paper
55cm × 43cm
Private Collection, Charles Marks

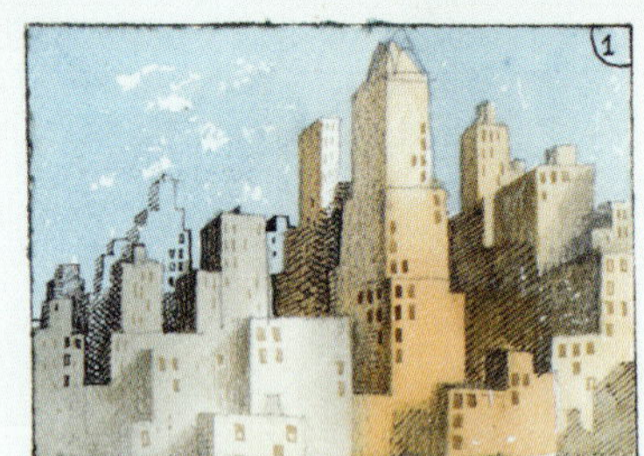

1 The New York skyline fills the screen...

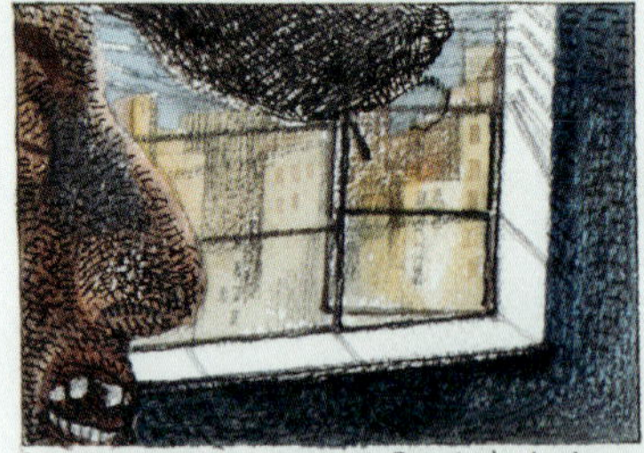

2 TRACK BACK TO TAKE IN Spanky's bedroom ...that of typical American teenager of 1950's but not well-off...

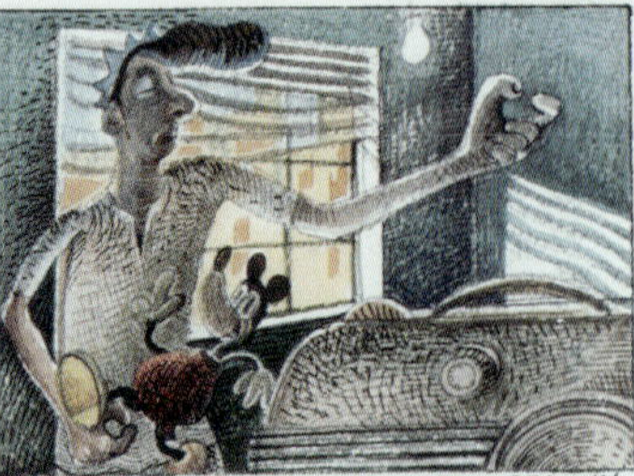

3 'All Shook Up' on bedside radio. SPANKY, in sagging boxer shorts and worn sloppy Joe, miming to ELVIS. Rapping noise on sound... SPANKY, eyes shut, is oblivious...

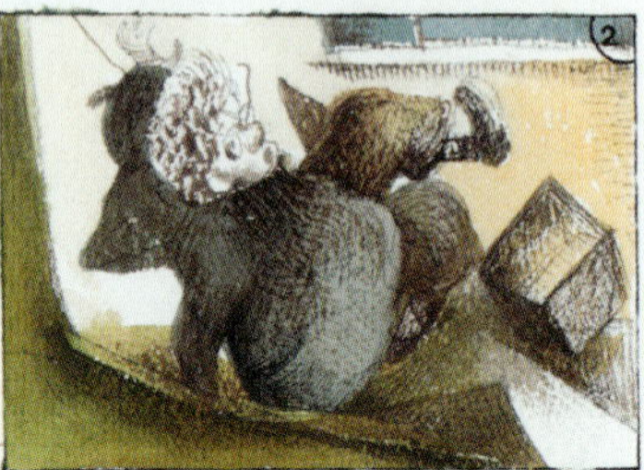

6 CUT TO: EXT. BACKYARD. HECTOR stumbles backwards onto sawn-off BOAC 'Fly To USA' hoarding nailed to pole...

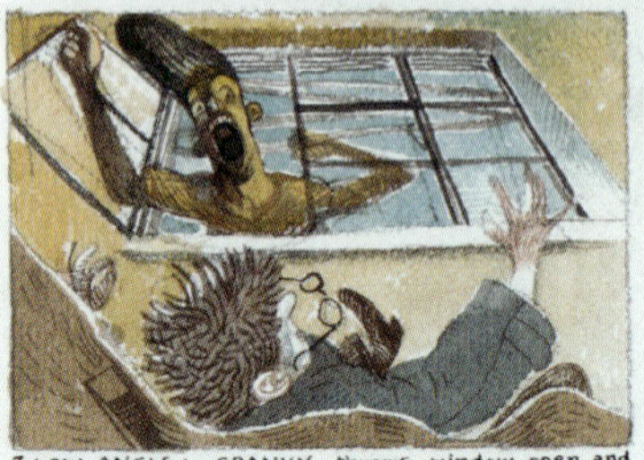

7. LOW ANGLE : SPANKY throws window open and gives runt a bawling out...

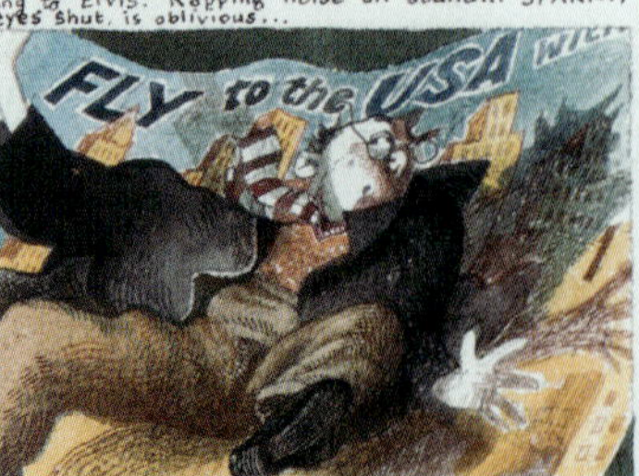

8. SPANKY'S P.O.V. HECTOR sprawled across N.Y. skyline.

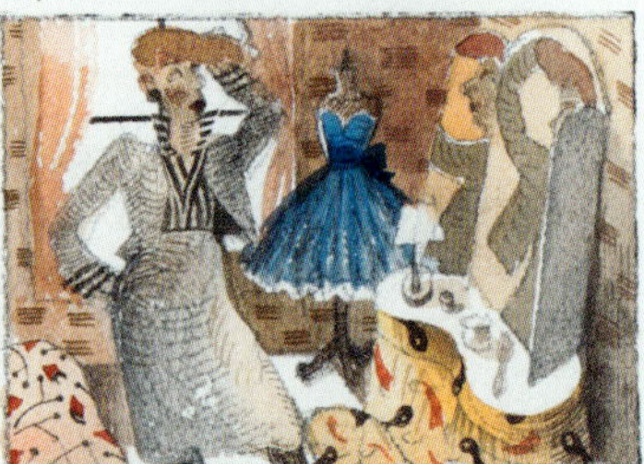

11. PULL OUT: LUCILLE gets up, puts jacket on, checks her appearance. More motorbike horn on SOUND...

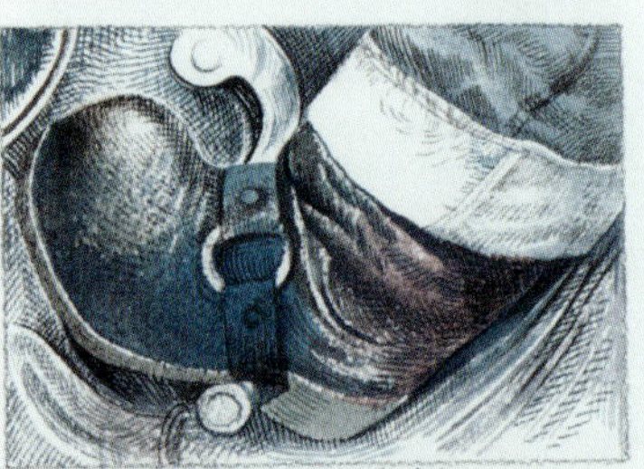

12. CUT TO: TERRY revs up motorbike.

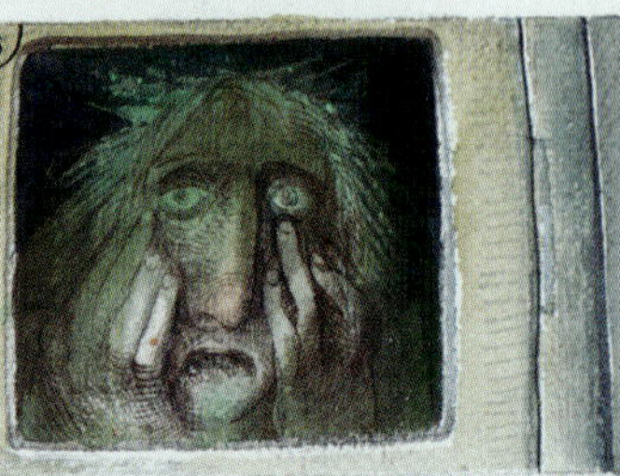

13. EXT: DARKWOOD CRESCENT... MRS McCANN'S face pressed against rear window of ambulance as it pulls away...

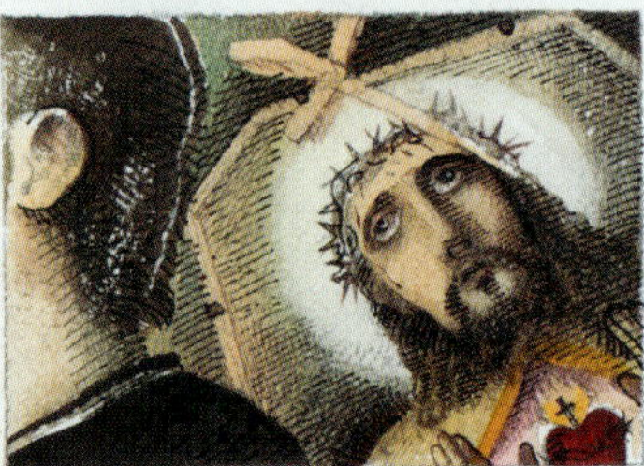

16 ...holy pictures askew...clothes scattered everywhere...

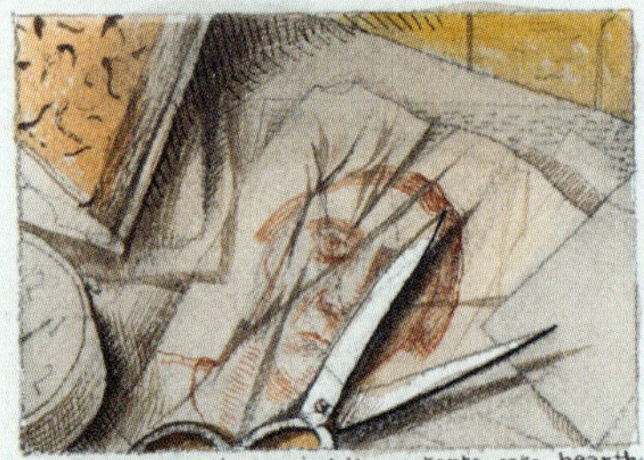

17 ...Phil's portfolio spewing its contents onto hearthrug... C.U. red chalk drawing of Mother, face gouged with scissors...

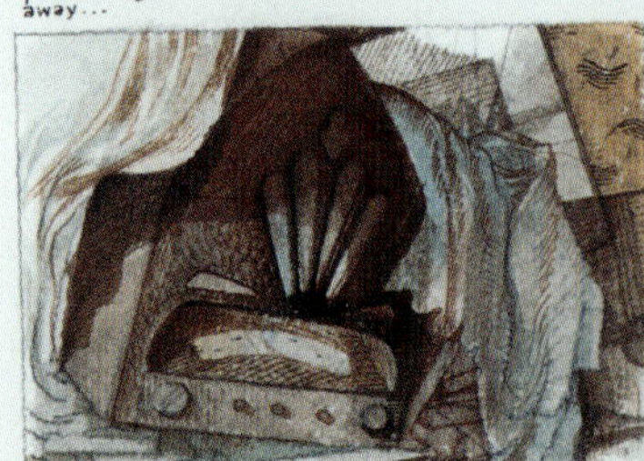

18. 'All Shook Up' on radio...

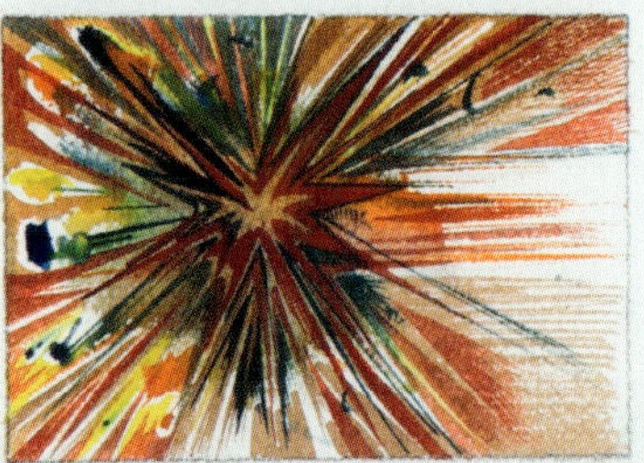

21. Screen explodes into opening titles...

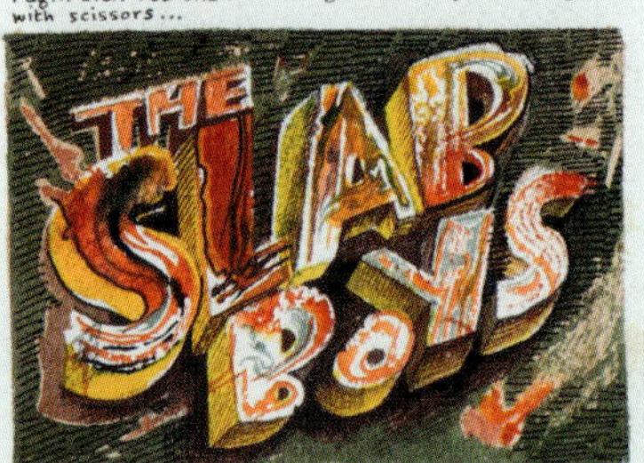

22 ...bring up rhythmic 'clank clank' of factory looms on sound under 'All Shook Up'...

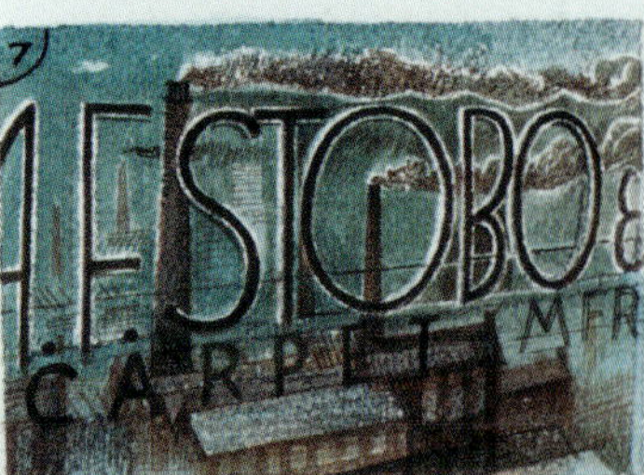

23. FADE UP to early morning factory & sign...

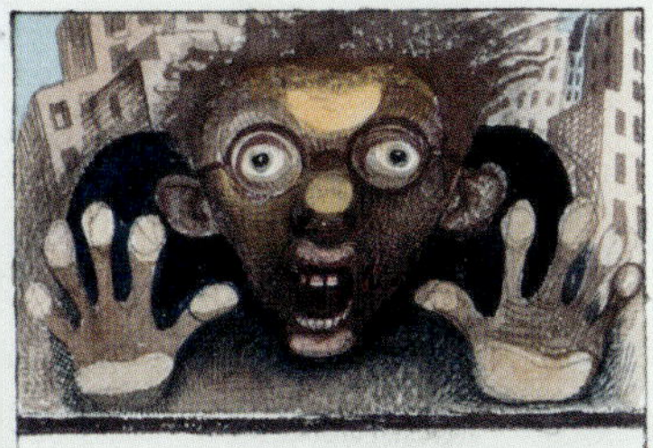

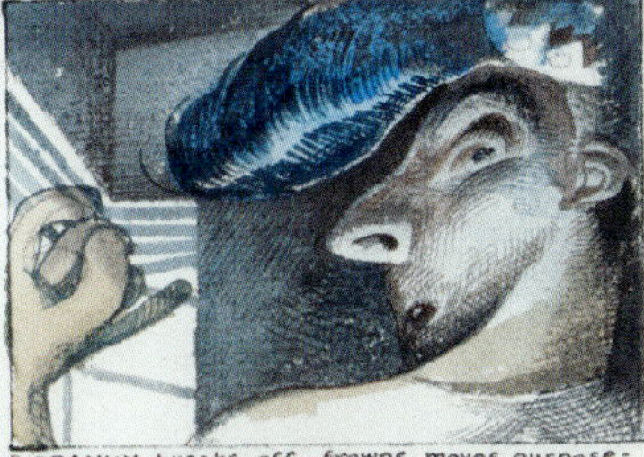

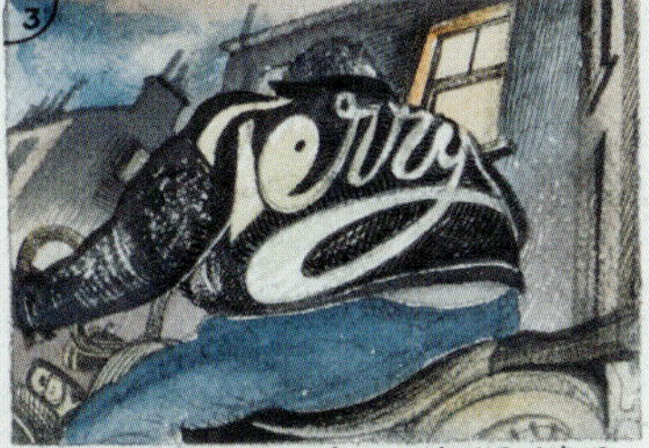

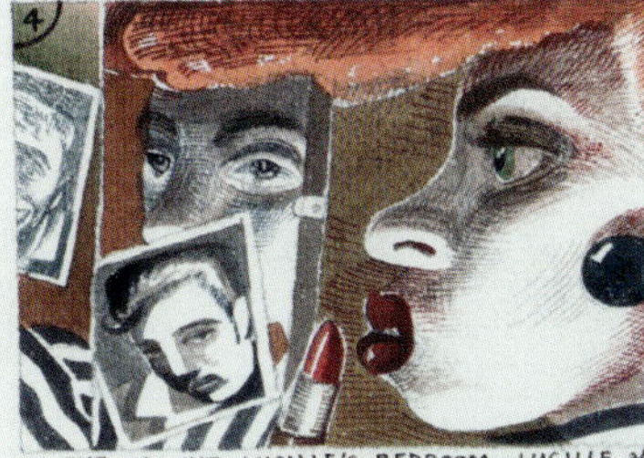

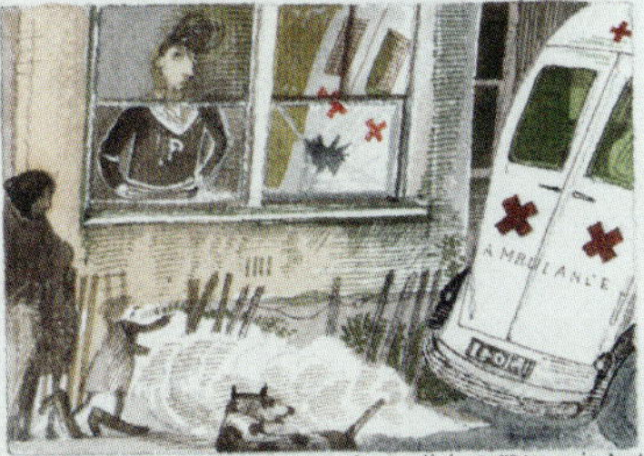

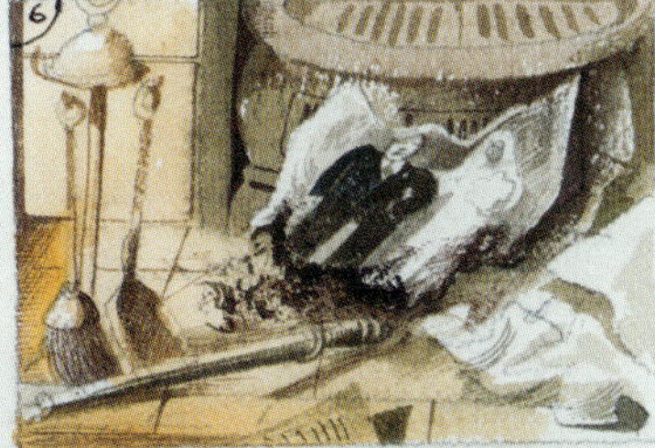

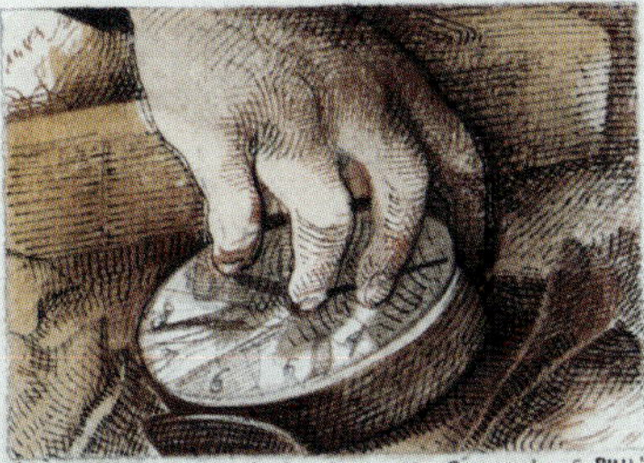

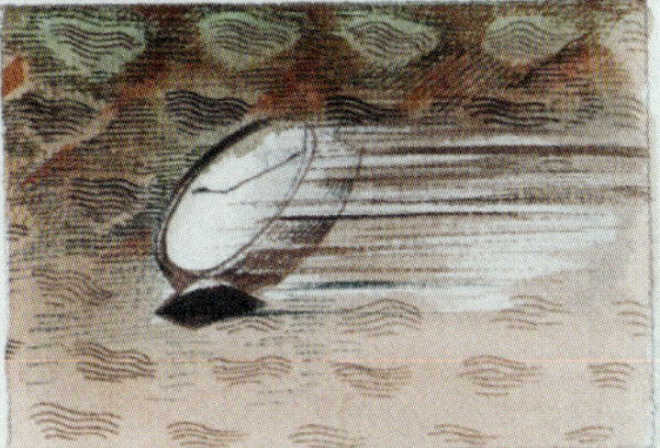

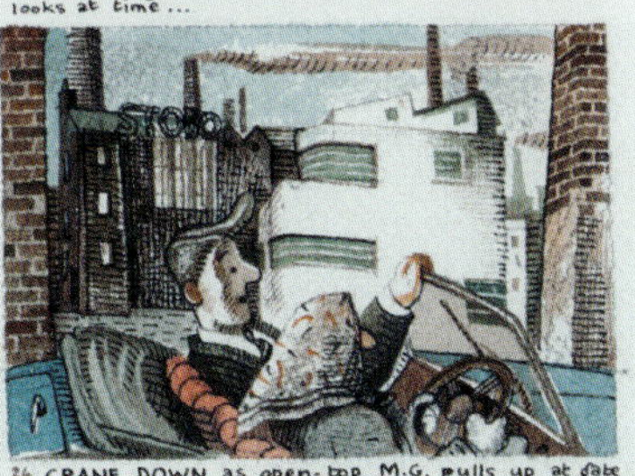

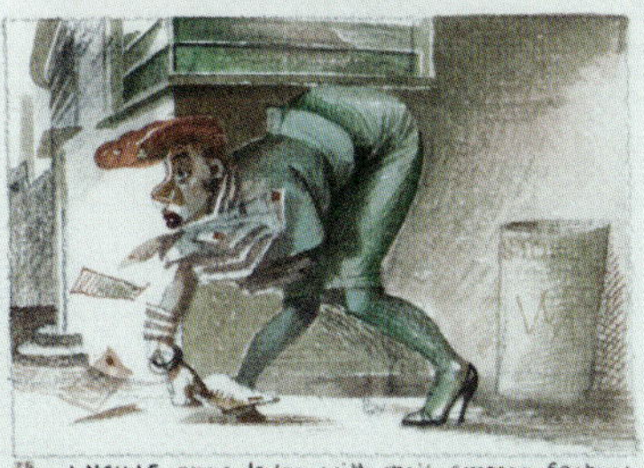

The Slab Boys film storyboards, about 1995–97
Ink and watercolour on paper
68cm × 81cm
Private Collection, Charles Marks

Byrne adapted and directed *The Slab Boys* film,
released in 1997. These storyboards show his
meticulous attention to detail; he drew and
painted each scene, while also producing stage
sets and animated titles.

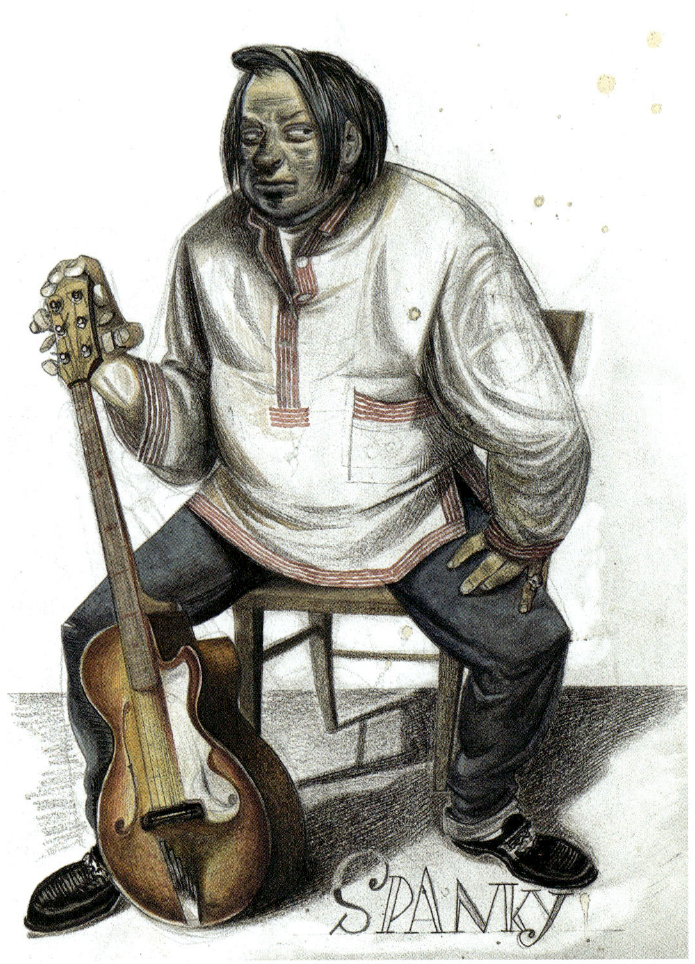

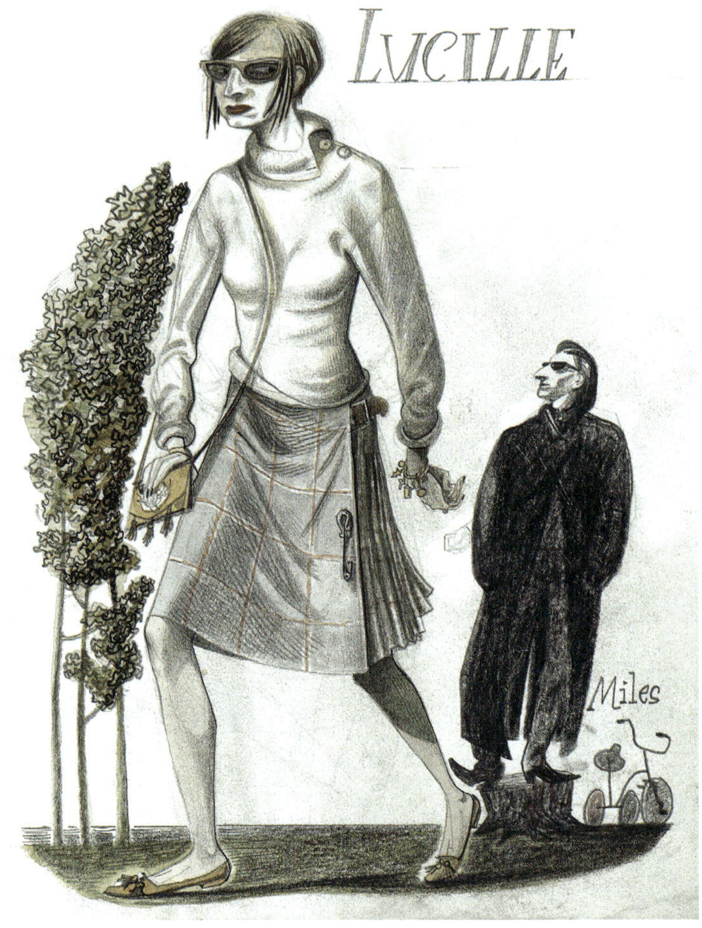

Spanky and Lucille, 2006
Mixed media on paper, 29.21cm × 21.59cm
Private Collection, Charles Marks

Sketches of the characters Spanky and Lucille from Byrne's play *Nova Scotia*, the fourth part of *The Slab Boys* story.

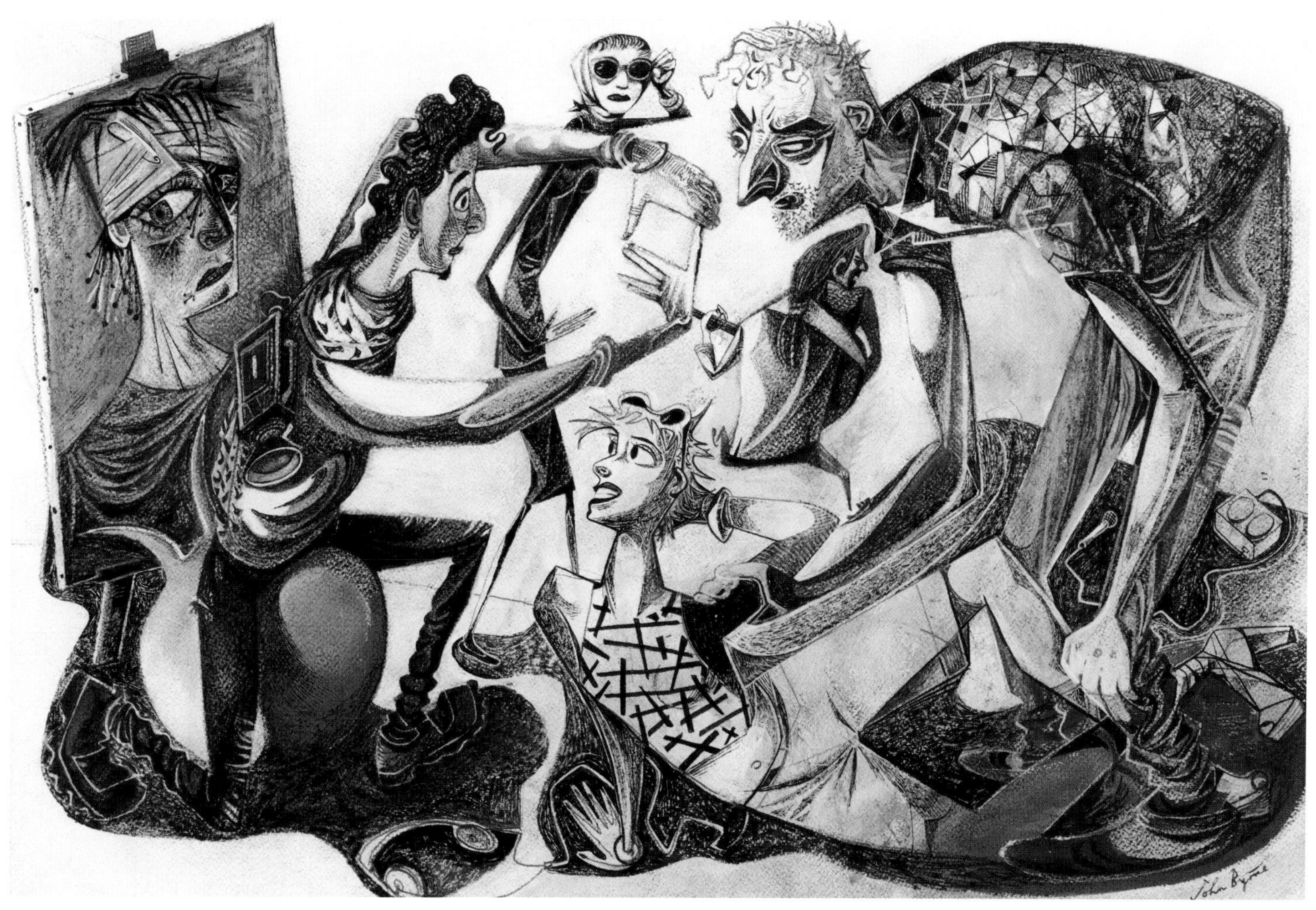

Nova Scotia, about 2008
Graphite, watercolour on paper, 58cm × 72cm
Private Collection, Charles Marks

Nova Scotia is the fourth part of *The Slab Boys* 'trilogy'. Set 30 years after *The Slab Boys*, this sees three of the original characters, Phil, Spanky, and Lucille, reunited.

Writing for the BBC

Bill Bryden, then Head of Drama at the BBC, approached Byrne to write a TV series. There was one stipulation – it had to be called *Tutti Frutti*. Byrne agreed, but only if he wrote every episode, with no edits. Bryden consented and an iconic TV show was born.

Set in Glasgow, it follows the exploits of The Majestics, a fictional Scottish rock 'n' roll band preparing to go on a twenty-fifth anniversary tour when their singer dies in a car crash. When the singer's brother comes home for the funeral, the band try and recruit him for the tour.

The series featured a host of Scottish acting talent while helping to launch the careers of Robbie Coltrane (who played both brothers) and Emma Thompson. The show was so successful a publication and soundtrack were released. *Tutti Frutti* was later adapted for the stage in 2006 by the National Theatre of Scotland and performed at His Majesty's Theatre, Aberdeen.

In 1990 Byrne wrote *Your Cheatin' Heart*, which took Glasgow's country music scene as the background for a gripping, farcical, crime story. It featured singer-songwriter Eddi Reader and actor Tilda Swinton.

Both shows were watched by millions and have become cult classics. *Tutti Frutti* won six BAFTAs. There was no award for best writer, but Byrne and Sandi Anderson won the Best Graphics award.

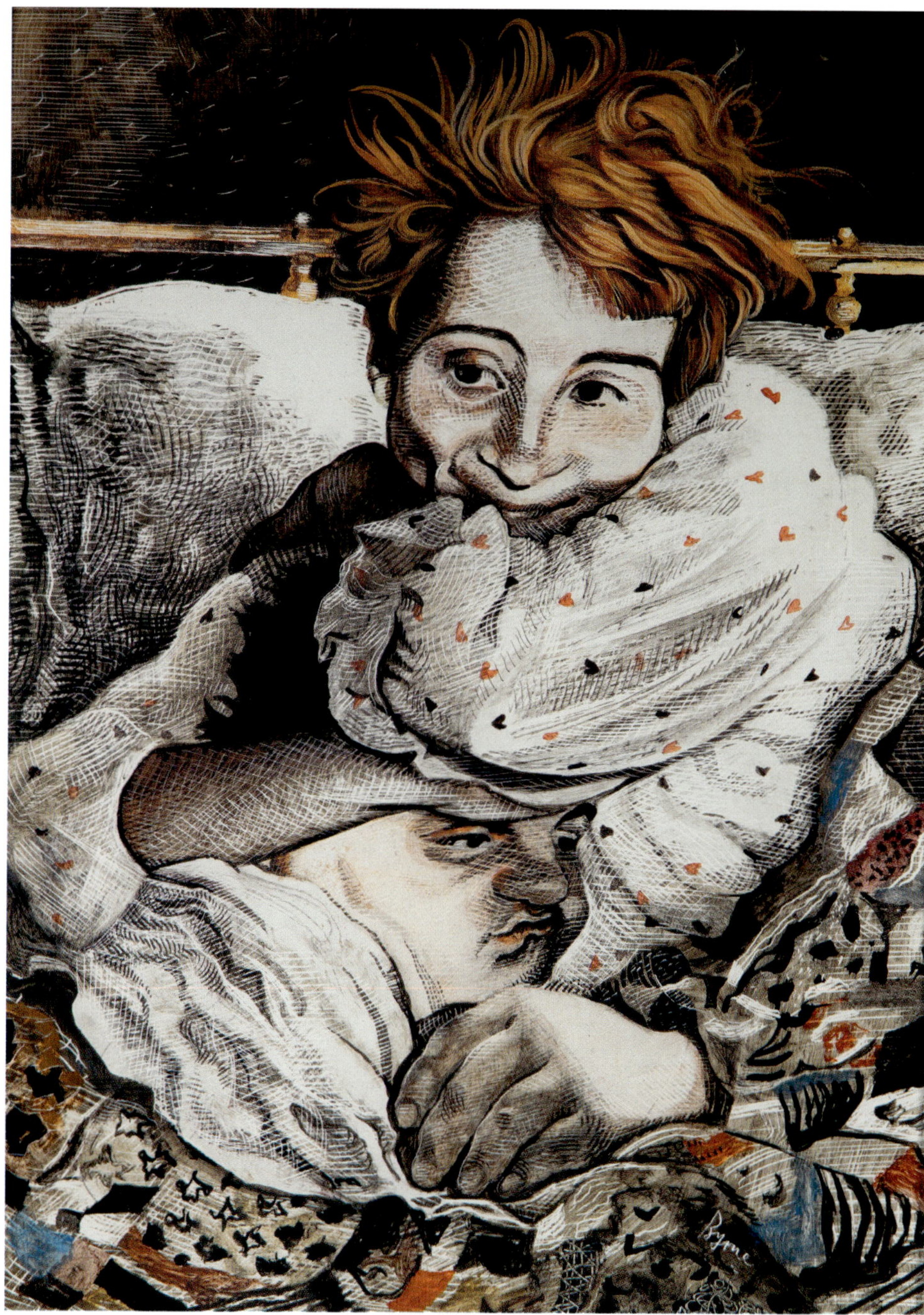

**Danny McGlone and Suzi Kettles
in Bed**, 1987
Gouache on white scraperboard
49cm × 40cm
Private Collection, Charles Marks

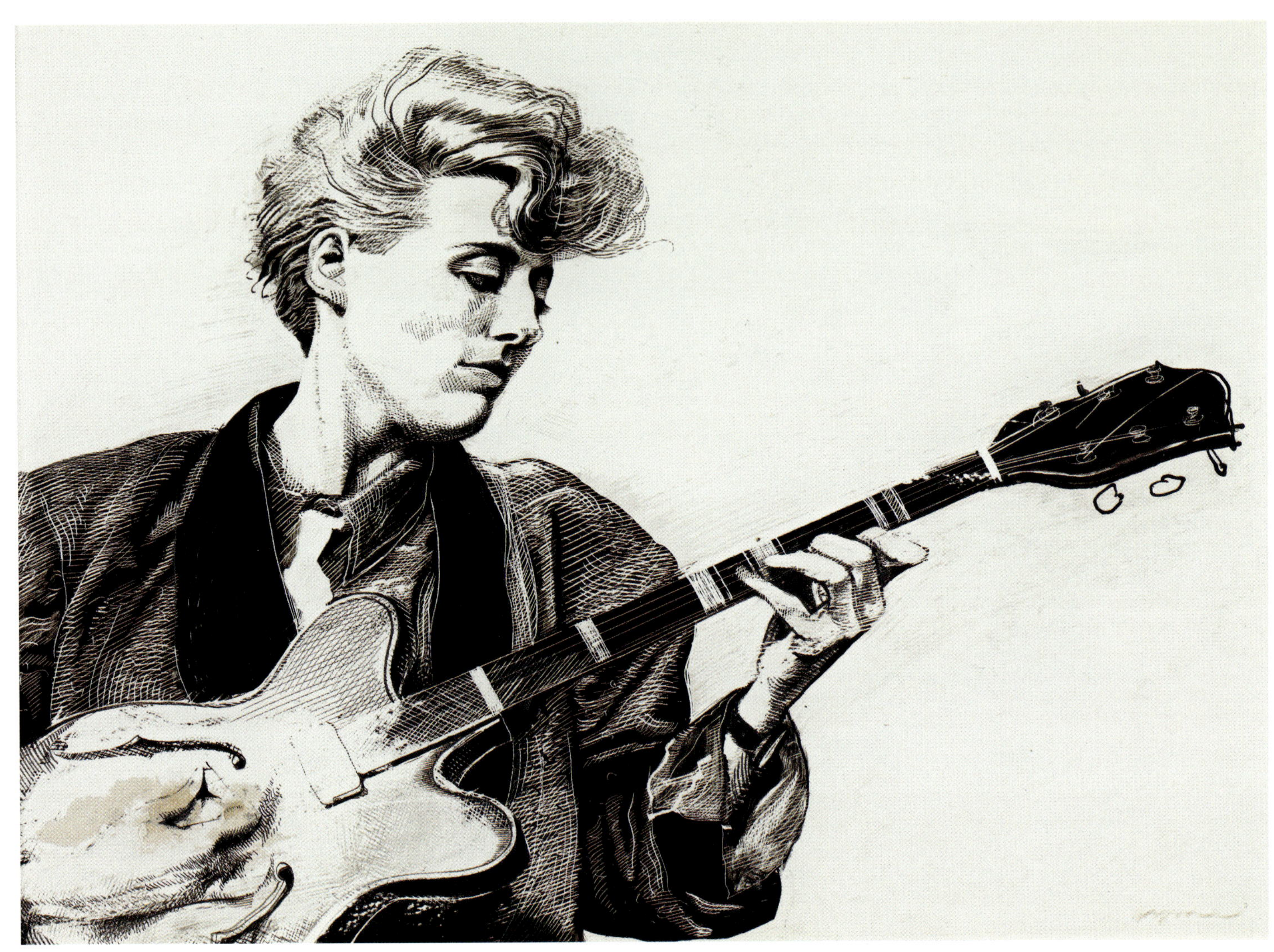

Emma Thompson as Suzi Kettles from Tutti Frutti, 1985–86
Watercolour, pen and ink, 20.9cm × 28.5cm
Lent by Emma Thompson

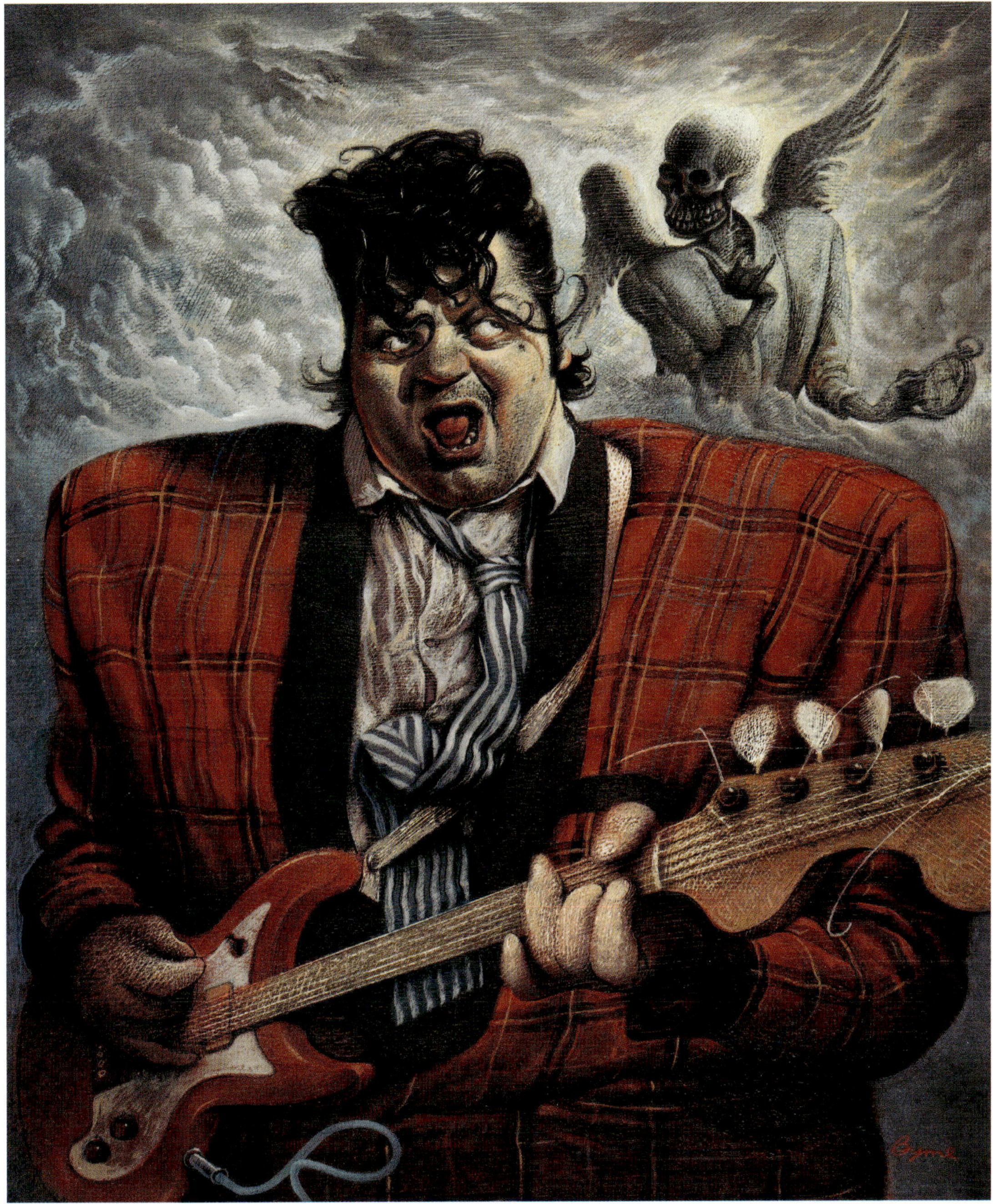

Robbie Coltrane as Danny McGlone in Tutti Frutti, 1985–86
Watercolour, pen and ink
31cm × 25.5cm (unframed)
Bought by Glasgow Museums, 1991
PR.1991.7

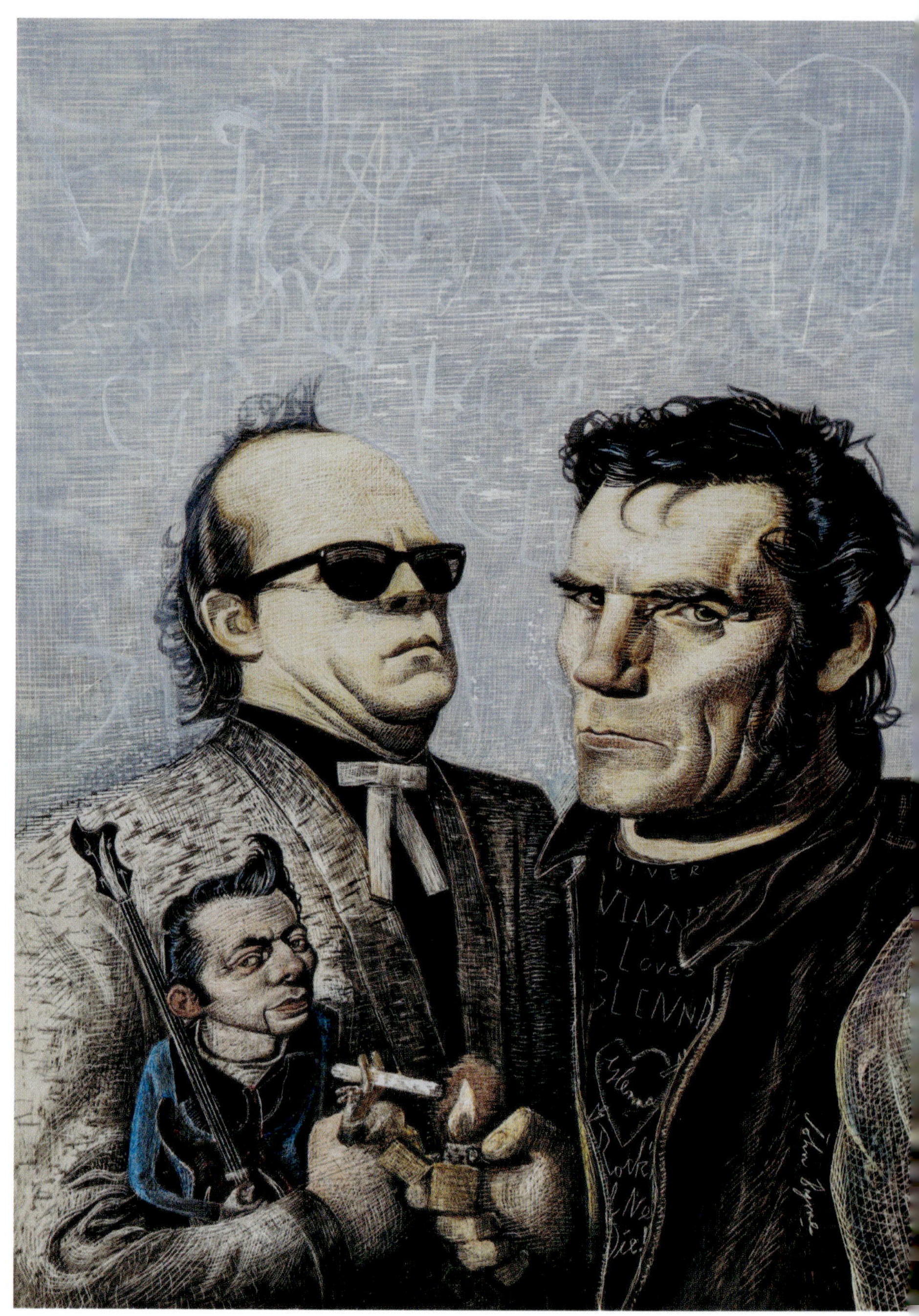

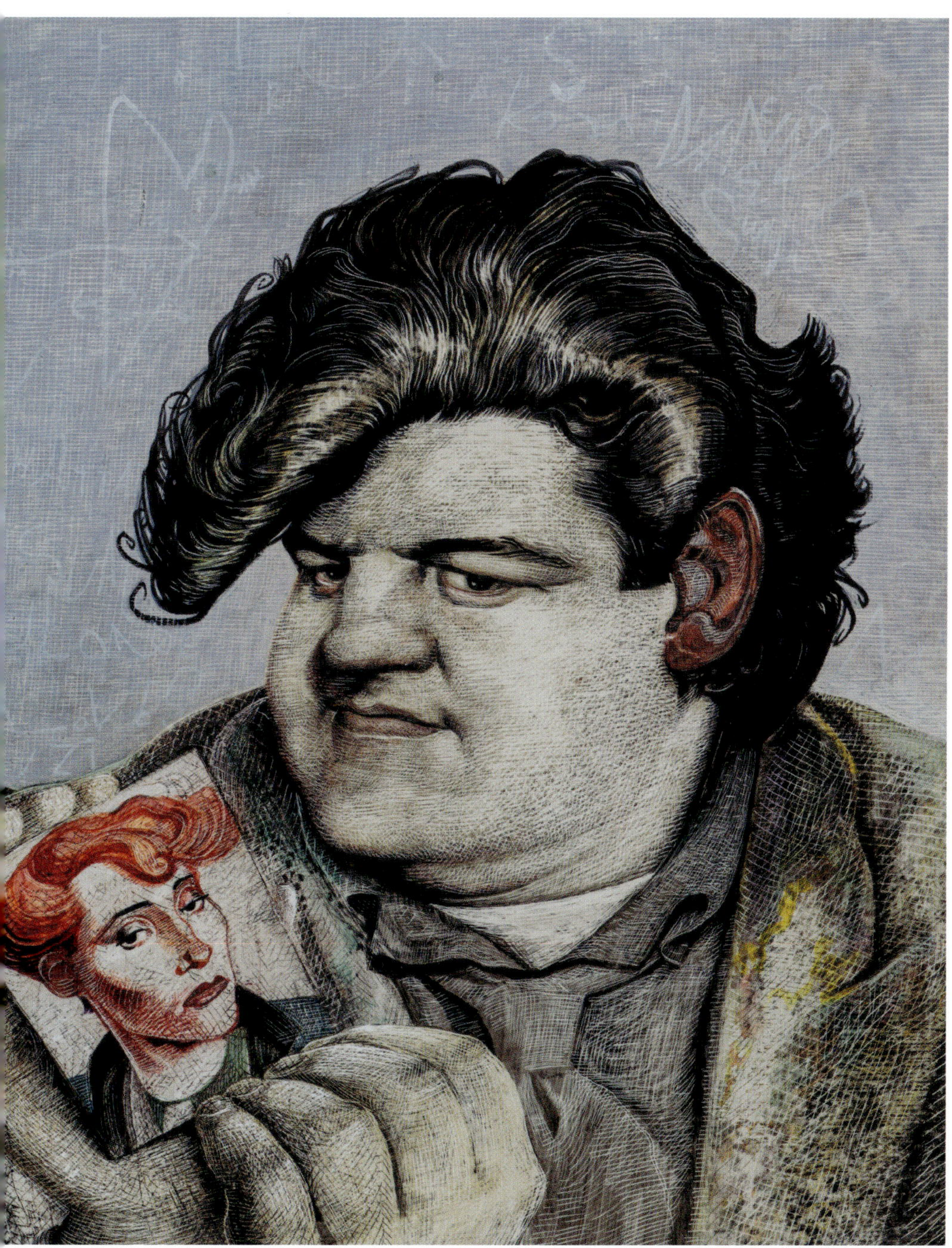

The Majestics, about 2009
Gouache on white scraperboard
49cm × 64cm
Private Collection, Charles Marks

This artwork was used for the DVD
release of *Tutti Frutti*. The Majestics are,
from left to right, Fud (Jake D'Arcy),
Bomba (Stuart McGugan), Vincent
(Maurice Roeves), Suzi (Emma Thompson)
and Danny (Robbie Coltrane).

Donald and Benoit

Donald and Benoit is a tale of friendship and hope between a boy, Benoit, and a cat, Donald, who live in the fictional Fishertown. Waiting anxiously for Benoit's dad to return from a dangerous fishing trip, the two of them get up to all kinds of adventures trying to make ends meet in a fishing town with no fish, while Donald dreams of joining the town's famous stage act, the Dancing Devildogs.

This was originally a bedtime story for Byrne's twins Honor and Xavier. The story changed every night as Byrne made up each adventure. He decided to write down one of the adventures, creating this children's book with wonderful illustrations.

Jeanine Byrne adapted and expanded the book into a play with Pitlochry Festival Theatre. It premiered as an audio play in December 2021, with physical stage performances planned.

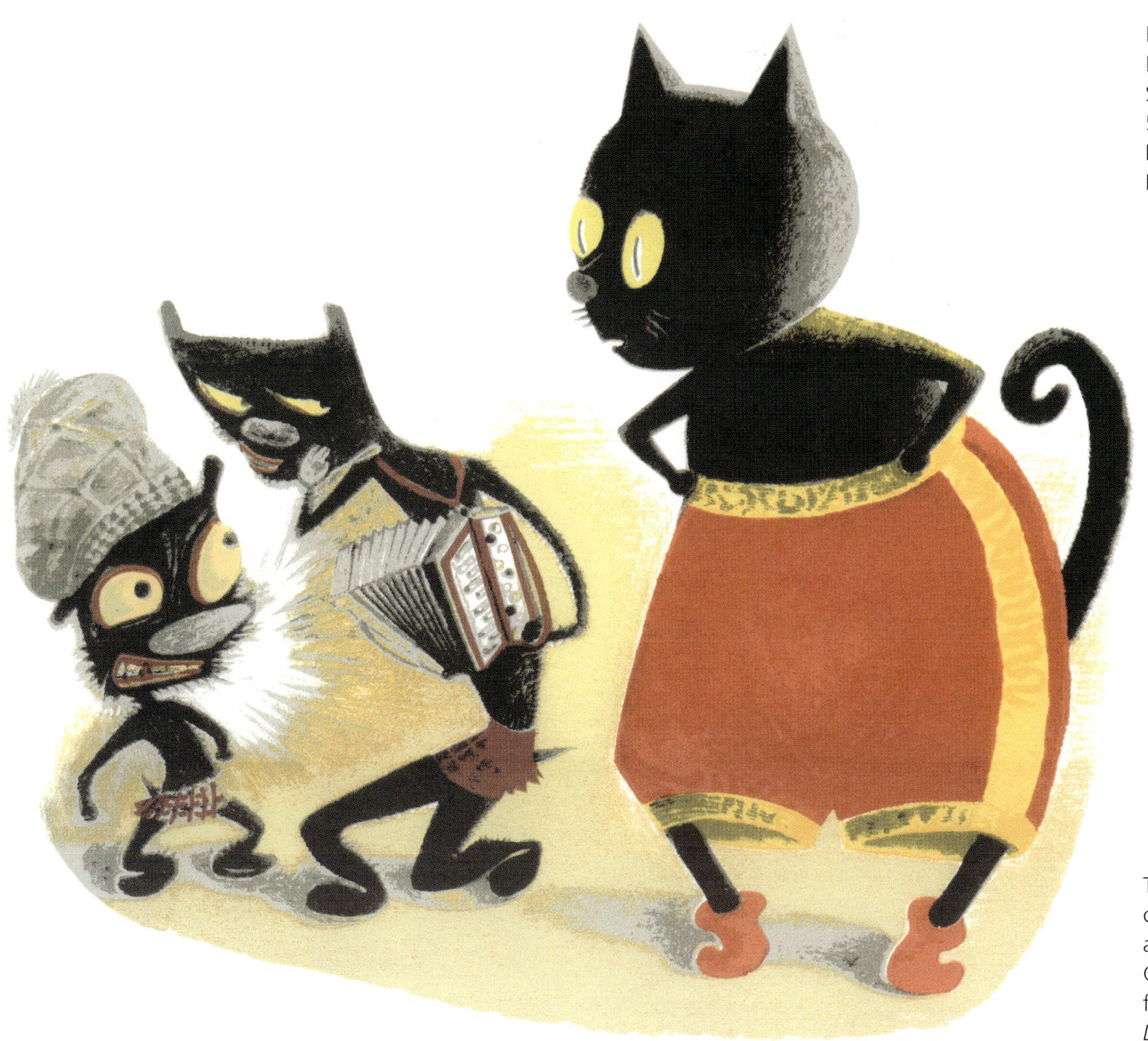

Donald Meets the Devildogs, 2020
Screenprint
53cm × 63cm
Lent by Glasgow
Print Studio

This screenprint was
created by Byrne and
a Master Printer at
Glasgow Print Studio
from images in
Donald and Benoit.

**Donald and the Dancing Devildogs
of Fishertown**, 2010
Mixed media, graphite, gouache,
coloured pencil, ink
66cm × 54cm
Lent by Andrew and Fiona Paterson

This is the alternative title and cover
Byrne considered for the book *Donald
and Benoit*.

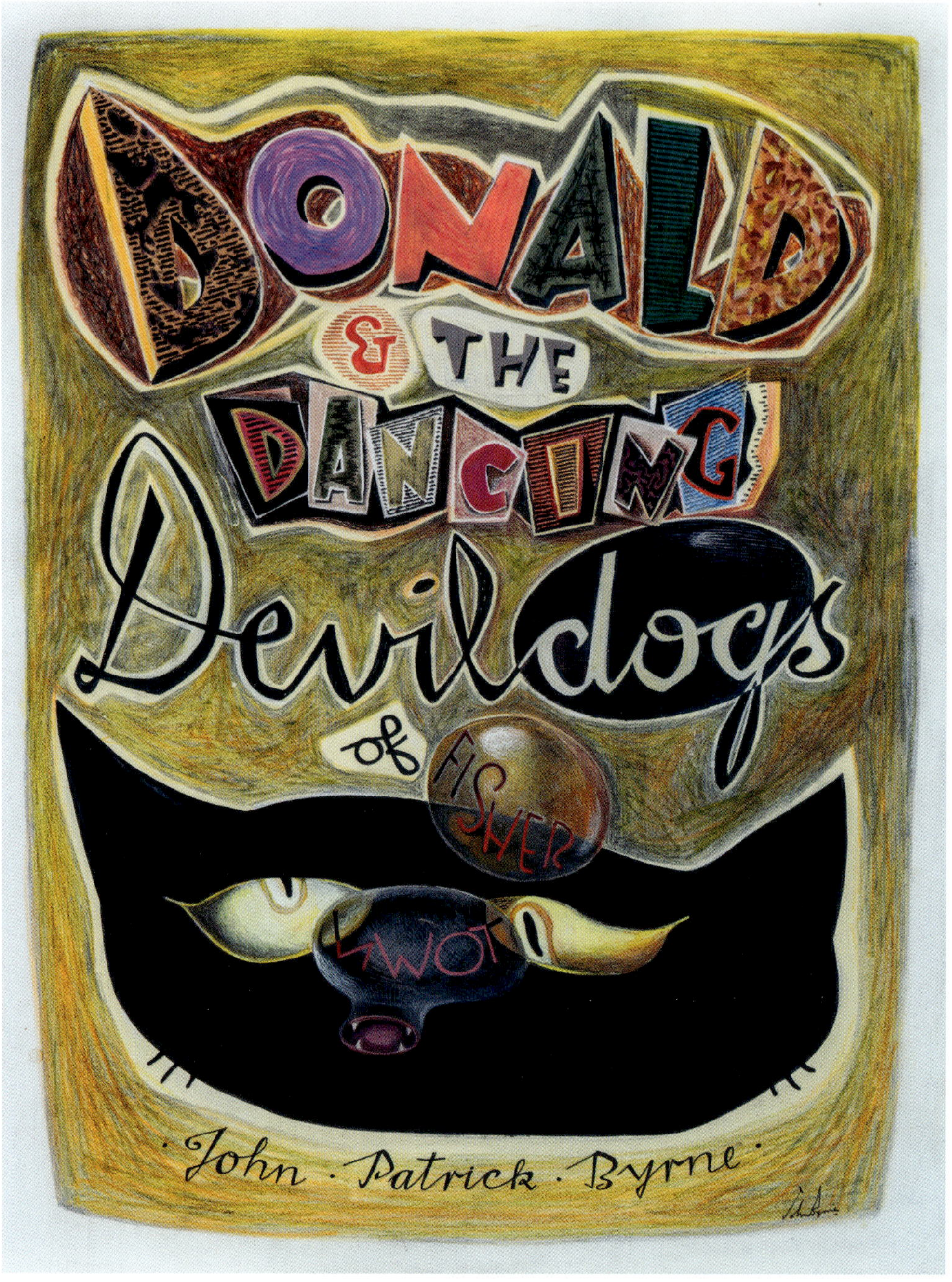

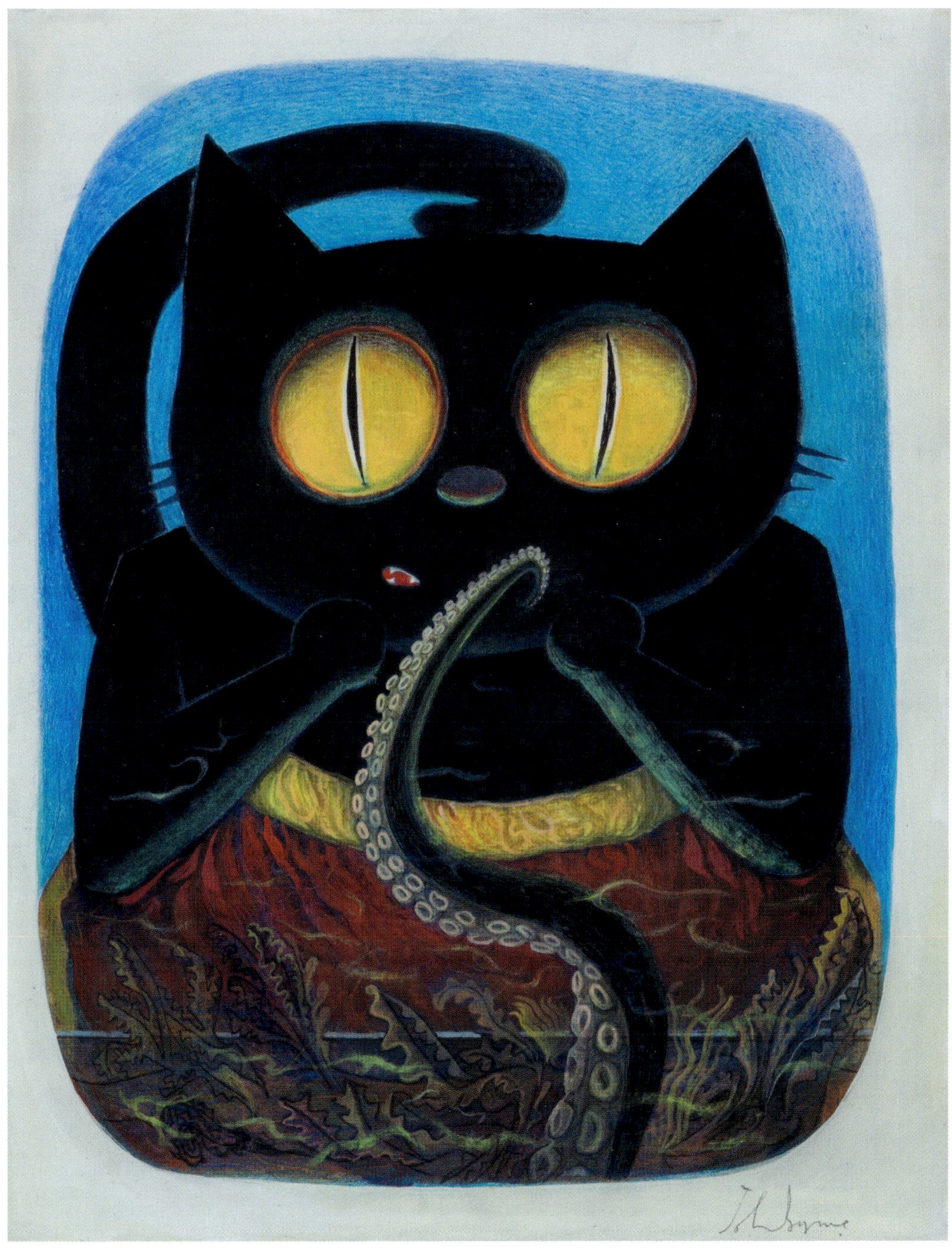

Study of Donald and Tentacle,
2010
Mixed media, watercolour,
gouache, conté
49.5cm × 40cm
Lent by Andrew and Fiona Paterson

Donald and Benoit –
On the way home, 2010
Mixed media, watercolour,
gouache, conté
50cm × 40cm
Lent by Ms Emily Walsh

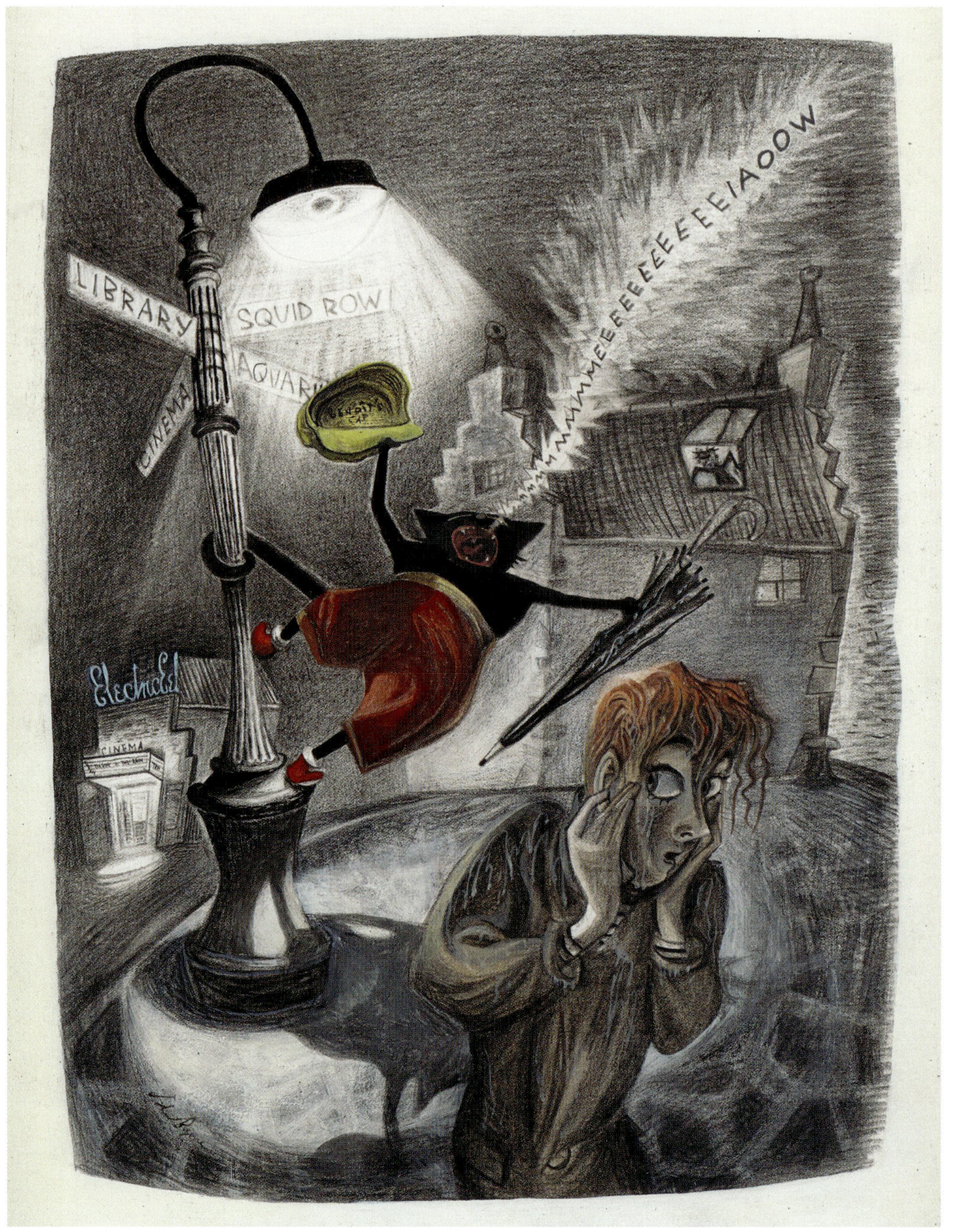

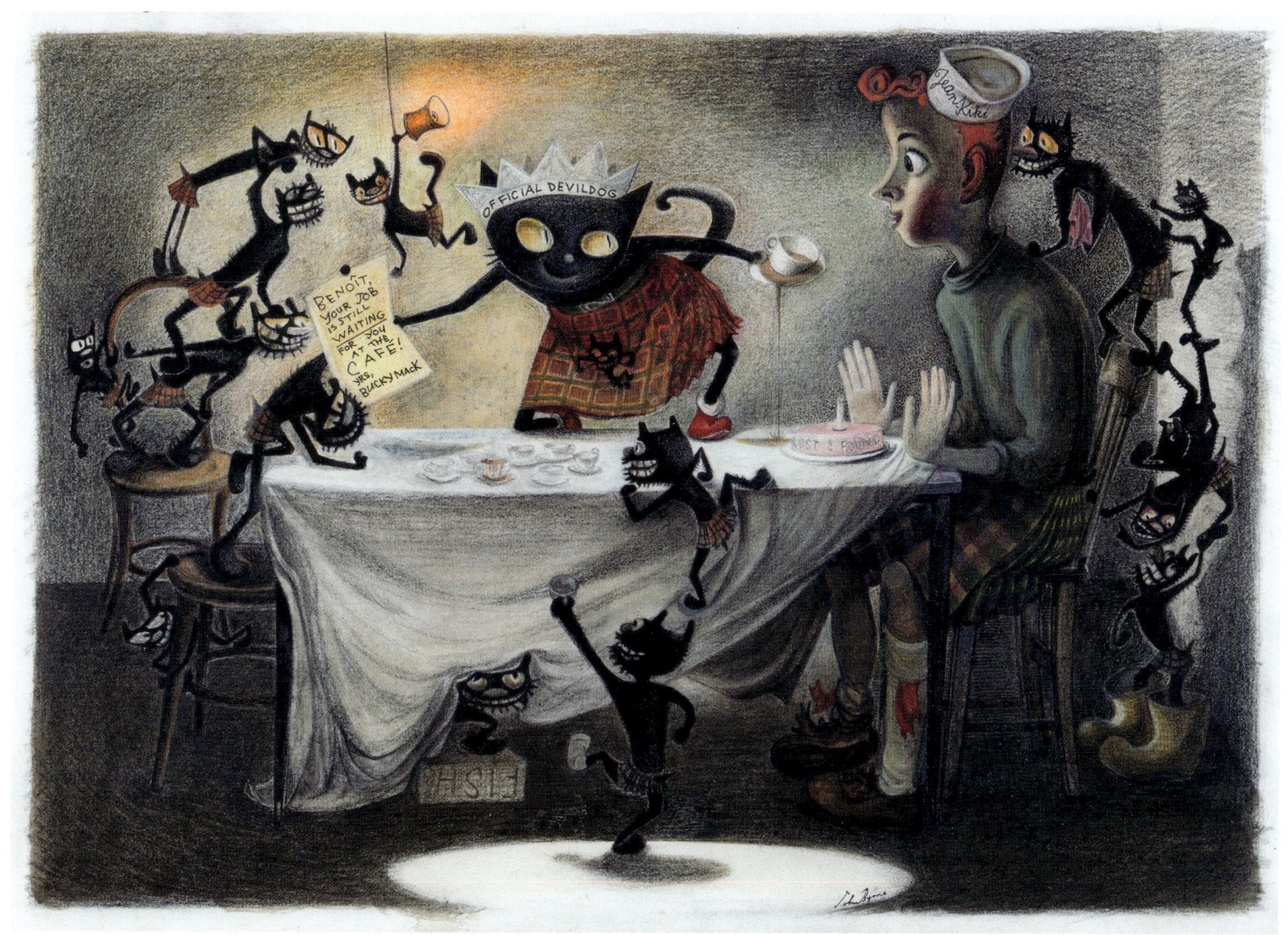

Donald and Benoit – The Banquet, 2010
Mixed media, watercolour, gouache, conté, 45.8cm × 60.5cm
Lent by Andrew and Fiona Paterson

Self portraits

Self-portraiture is a pillar of Byrne's artistic practice. Through this, you can see how Byrne has changed physically and artistically through the years. Personas, projected characters, and a growing sense of mortality become increasingly apparent.

A self portrait does not even have to be what is reflected in a mirror. There is a painting of a studio with personal objects in it, a painting of a paint palette with cigarette dowts, both unmistakably Byrne. Self-portraiture tells you something about the artist, even if this was not their intention.

It can be argued that all Byrne's artwork, plays, and TV shows are in some way autobiographical, and, as such, portraits of the artist – his depictions of quiffed Teddy Boys in his plays, or the Patrick characters surrounded by objects from Byrne's childhood.

The 1988 BBC *Arena* documentary *Byrne About Byrne* (written and directed by Byrne) is the ultimate meta self-portrait, with Byrne meeting himself at different ages. In it he says his life is 'scattered through plays and the television series like chaff'.

p. 66: *Self Portrait in Long Coat*, 1969, ink and wash, 39cm × 11cm, Private Collection; *Self Portrait in Gold-tinted Glasses*, 2016, oil on Arches paper, 56cm x 39cm, Private Collection; *Back to New York*, 2020, oil on linen, 70cm × 50cm, lent by Angus Franklin; *Cocky Self Portrait*, 2004, oil on board, 78cm × 78cm, lent by the Gilmour family, Edinburgh; *Self Portrait with Flat Cap*, 2008, oil, ink on board, 53.5cm × 43.2cm, Private Collection; *Dollar Point*, about 2009, oil on canvas, 90cm × 75cm, Private Collection, Charles Marks.

p.67: *The Drunken Sailor*, 2020, screenprint with watercolour, 83cm × 74cm, lent by Glasgow Print Studio; *Relaxez-Vous*, 2006, oil on board, 123cm × 92cm, lent by Mr Benny Higgins and Mrs Sharon Higgins; *Self Portrait Painting a Red Chicken*, 2008, oil, watercolour, ink on board, 48cm × 40cm, Private Collection; *Self Portrait with Skeleton and Cat*, 2008, watercolour, ink, conté and graphite on mount board and ink on paper; 53.5cm × 43.4cm, Private Collection; *Me and My Shadow*, 2019, oil on scraperboard, 28.6cm × 42.5cm, lent by Janet Mainnie/Private Collector; *Valiant*, 2017, oil on board, 74cm × 59cm, lent by Jamie Lonsdale.

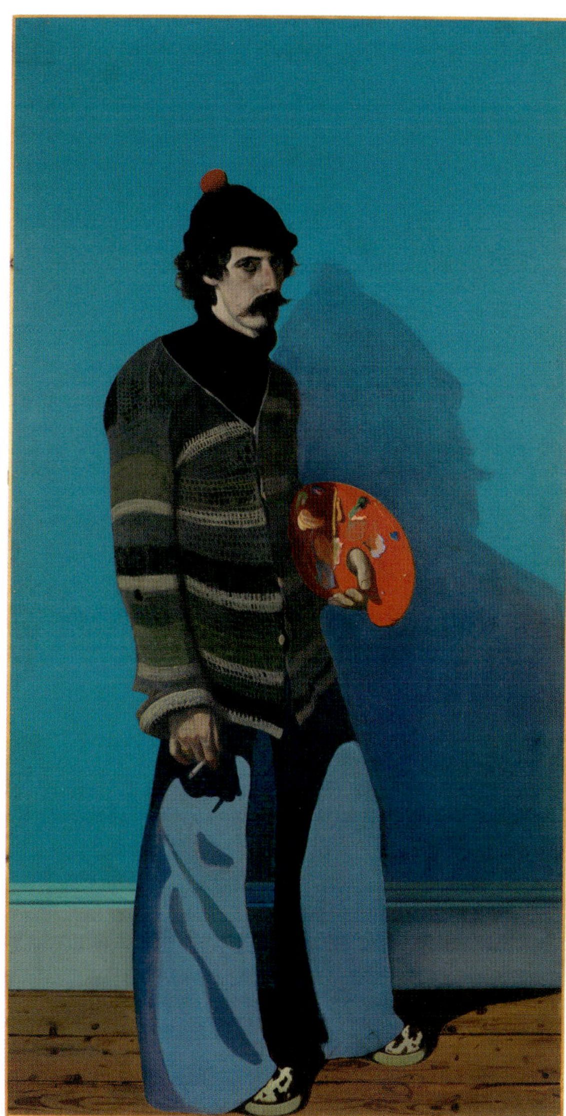

**Self-Portrait
with Red Palette**
(diptych), 1974–75
Oil and acrylic on
plywood
245.5cm × 123.5cm
(each panel,
unframed)
Glasgow Museums,
Scottish Arts
Council Bequest,
1997
3623.1 and 3623.2

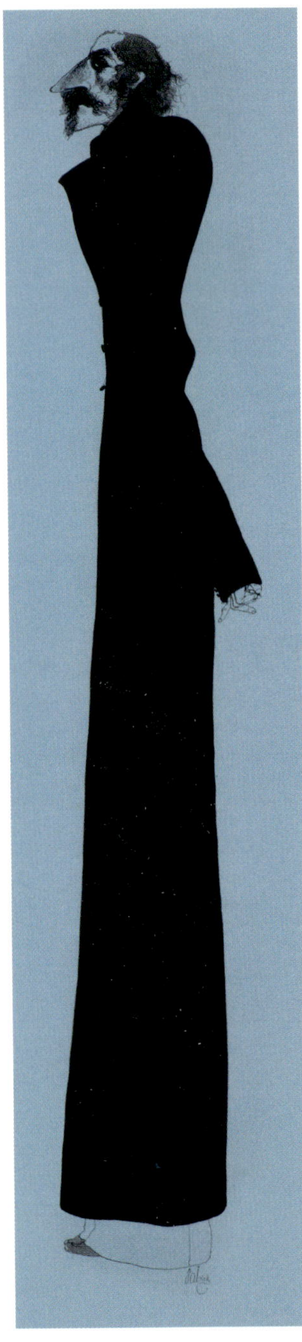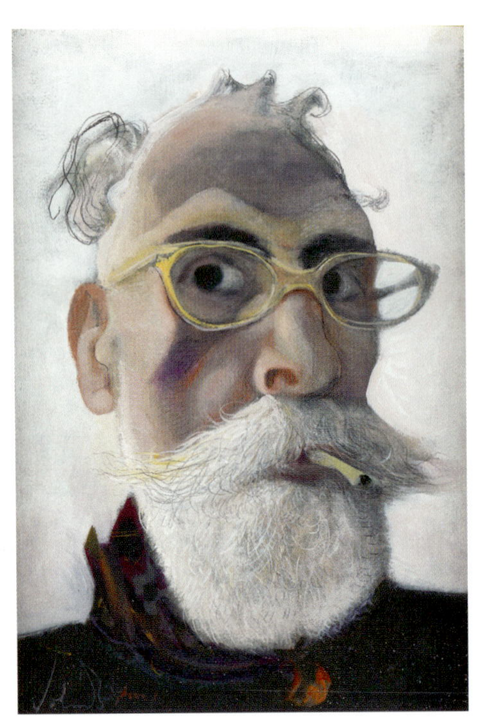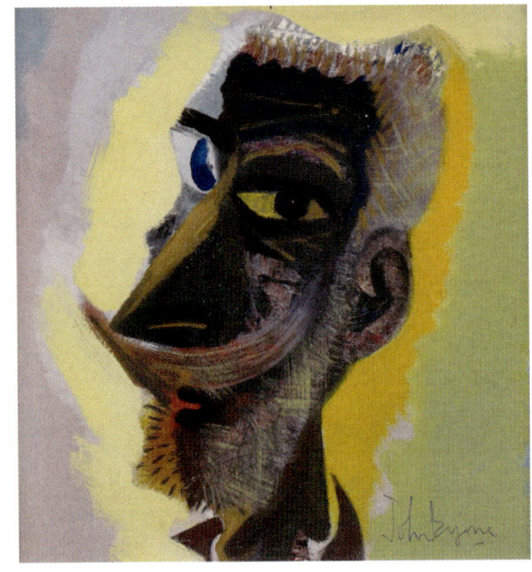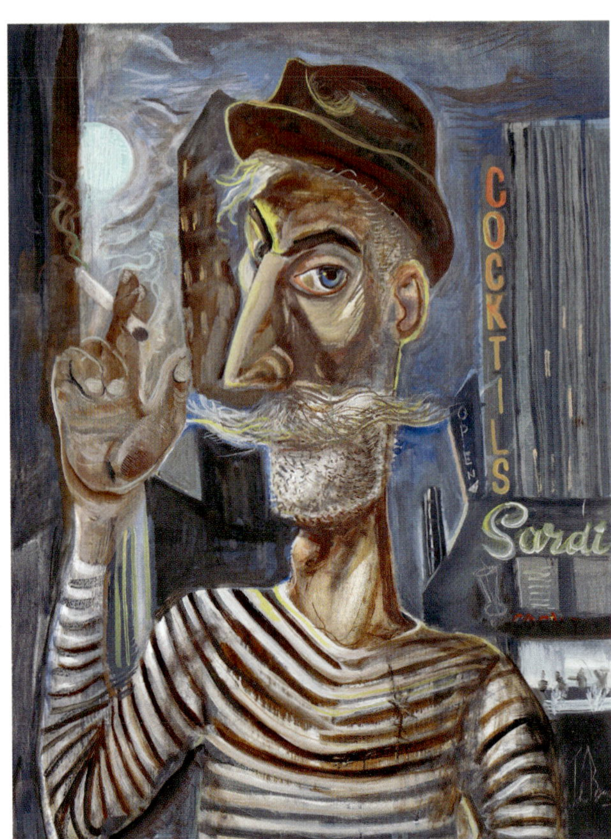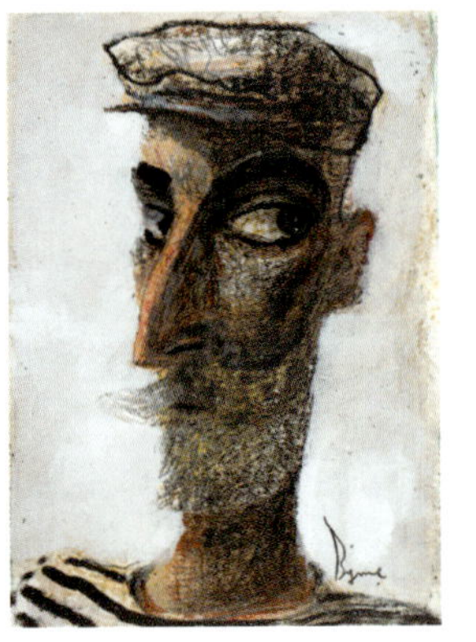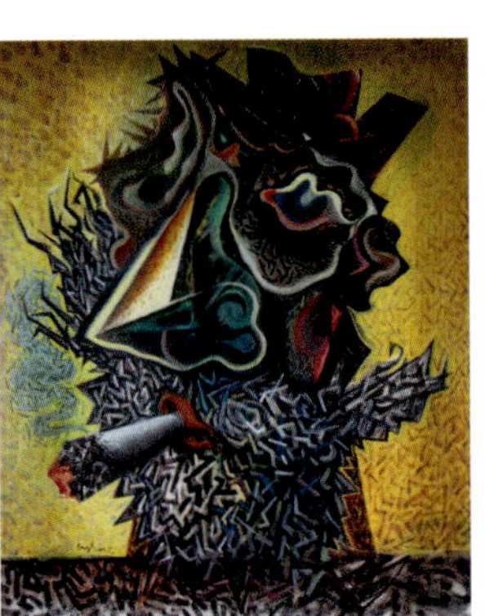

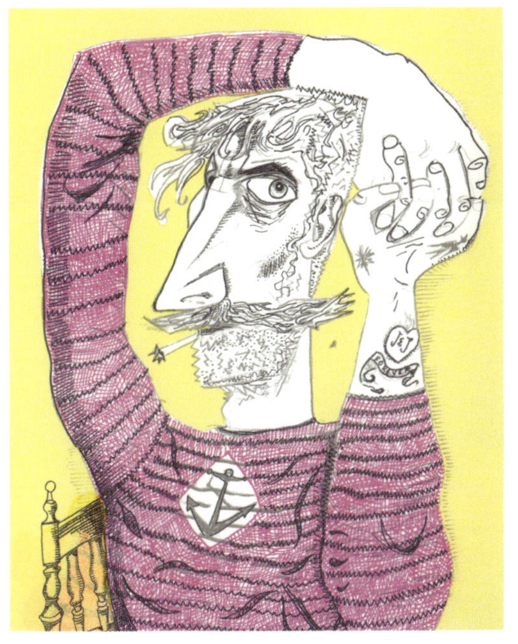

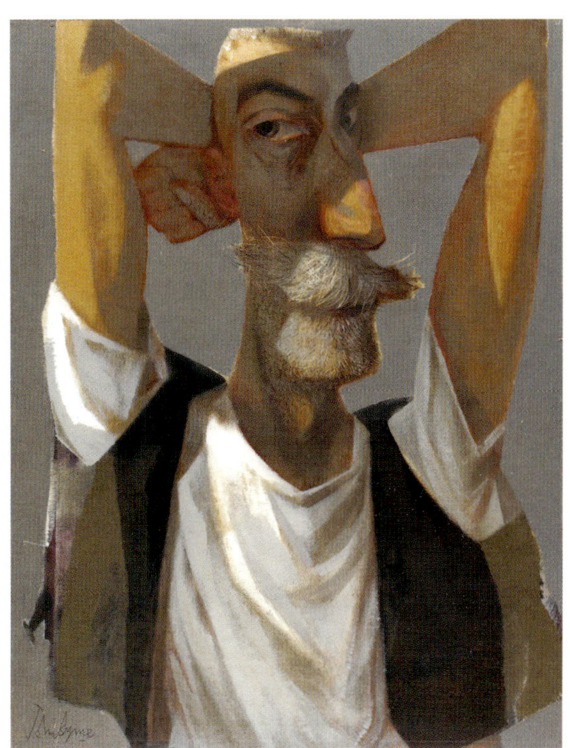

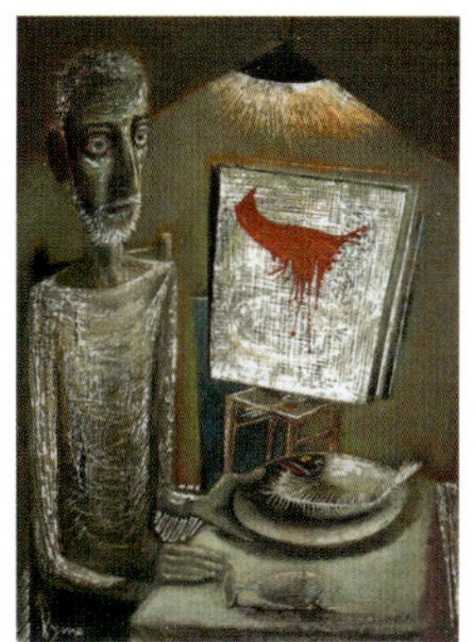

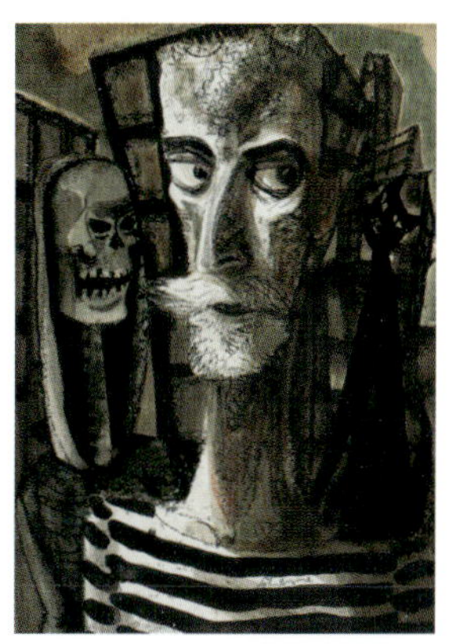

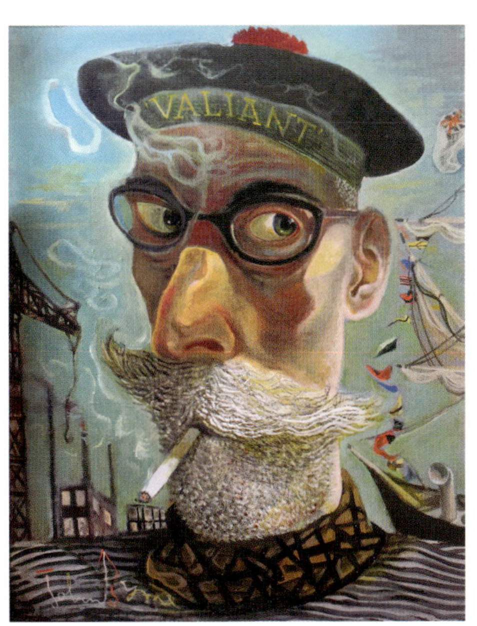
VALIANT

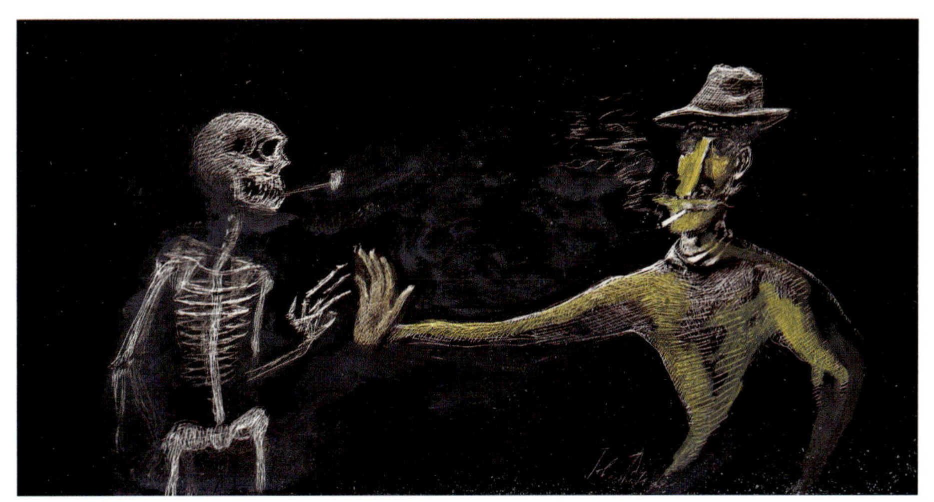

Self-Portrait in a Flowered Jacket,
1971–73
Oil on blockboard
161.5cm × 105.7cm
Lent by National Galleries Scotland
Presented by the Scottish Arts Council,
1997
PG3068

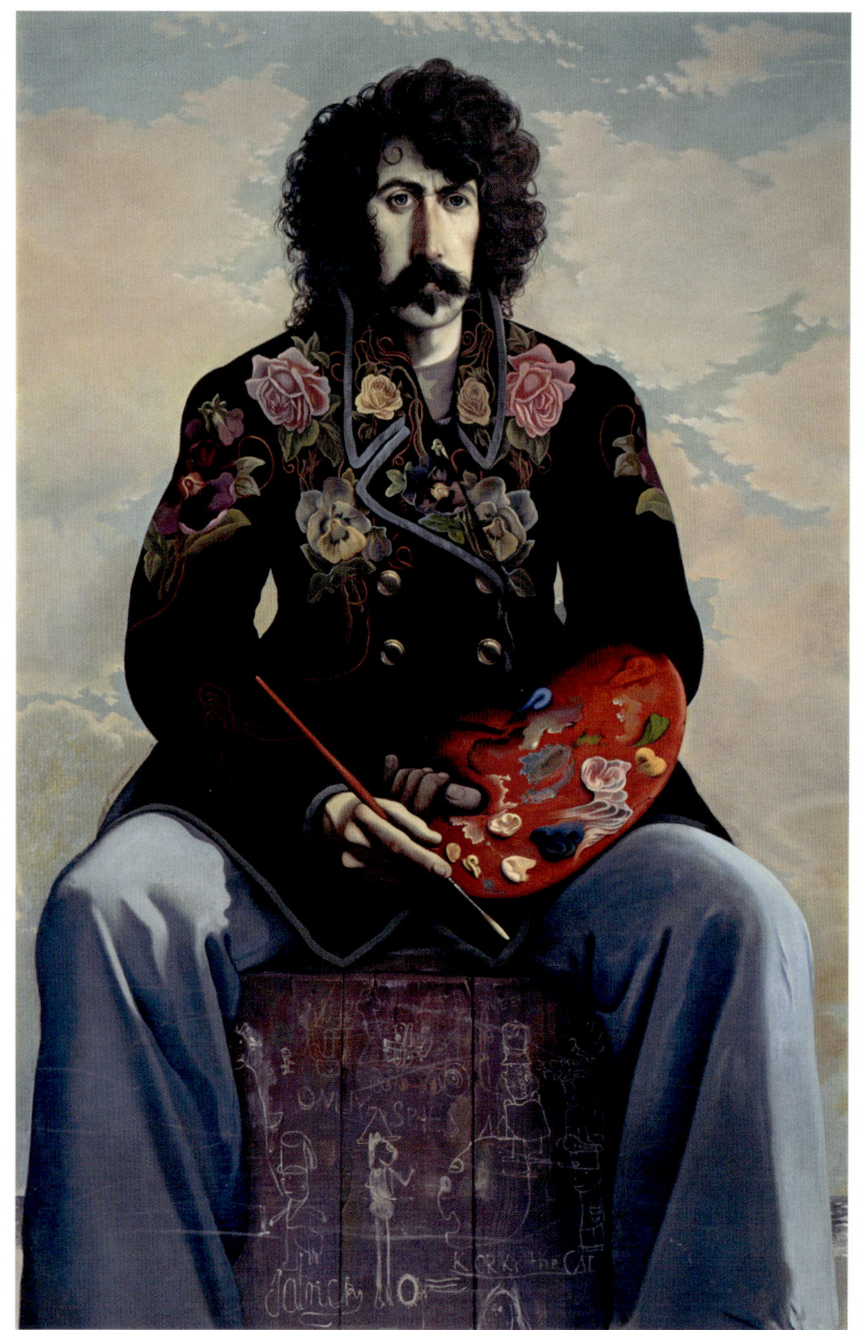

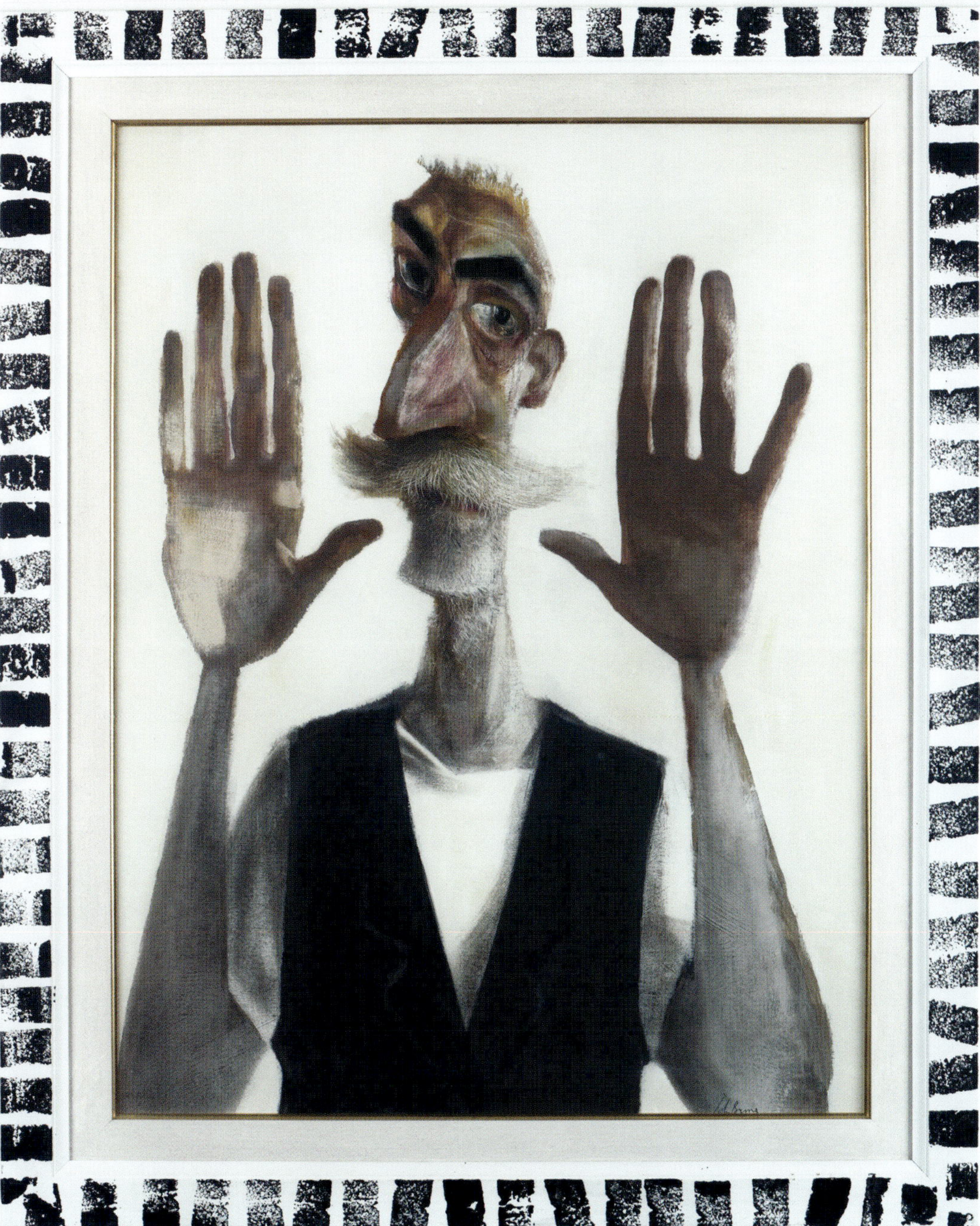

Hands Up, 2006
Oil on board, frame
painted by Byrne
149cm × 118cm
Lent by Andrew and
Fiona Paterson

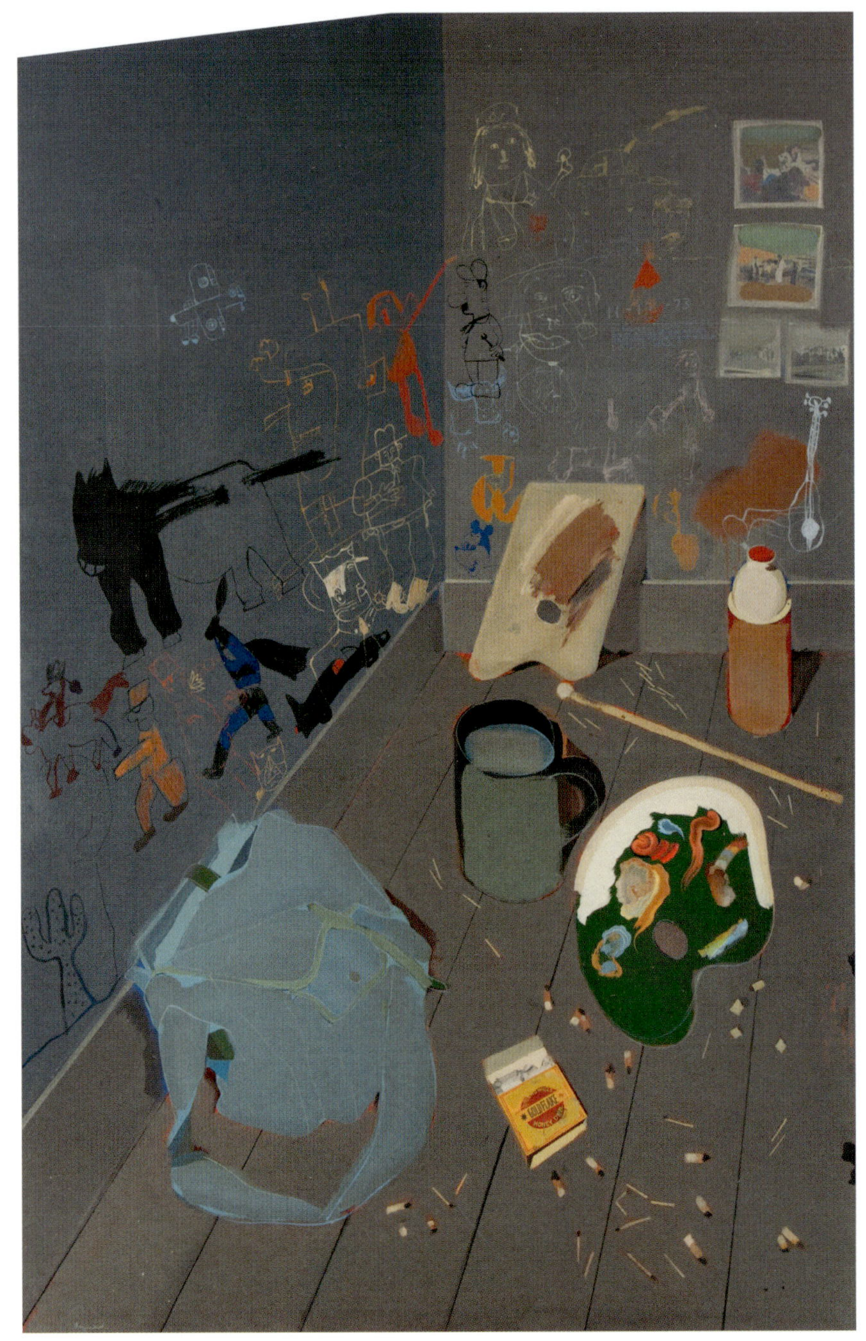

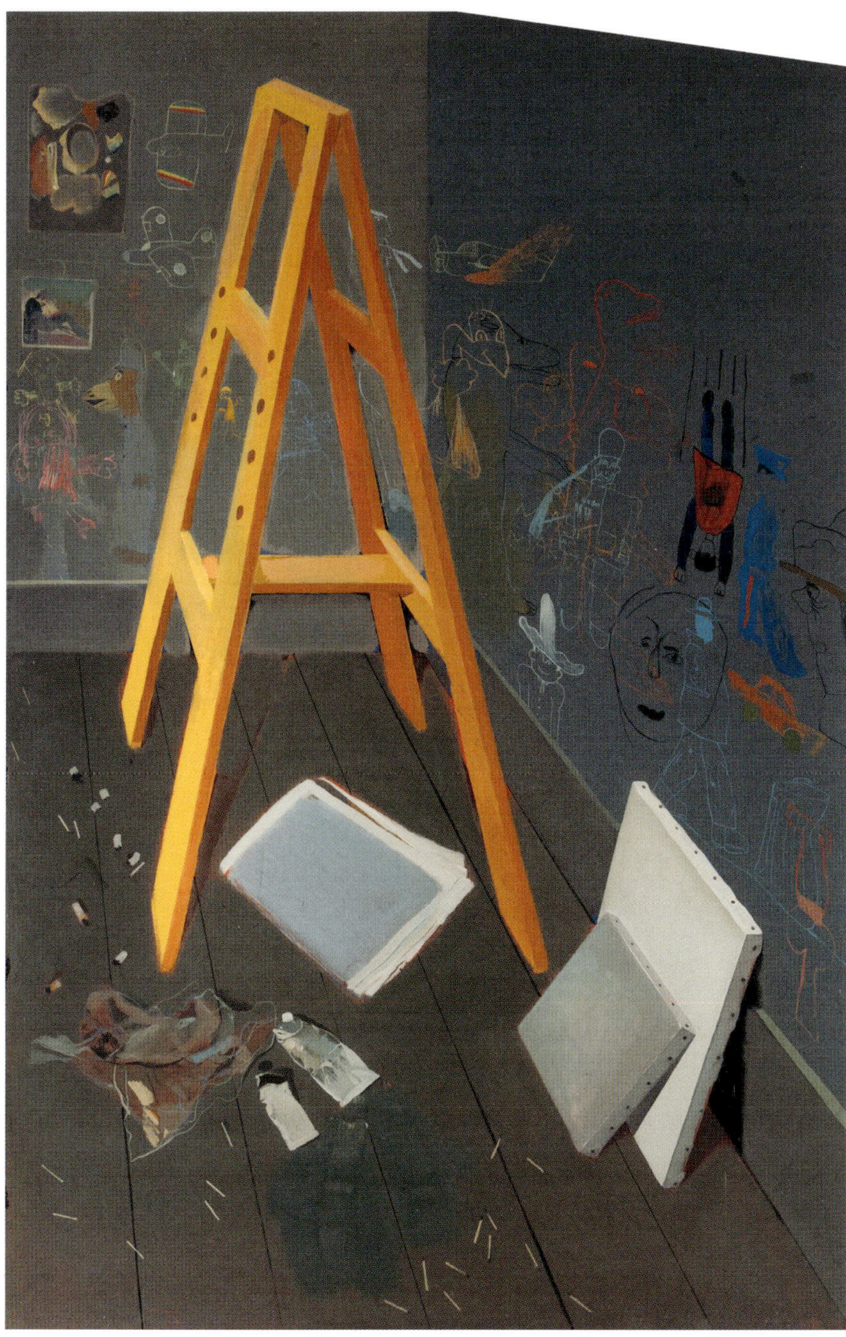

The Studio, 1975
Oil on plywood
197.2cm × 246cm
Renfrewshire Museums Collections,
lent by OneRen on behalf of
Renfrewshire Council
Purchased by the Art Fund
PCF 42

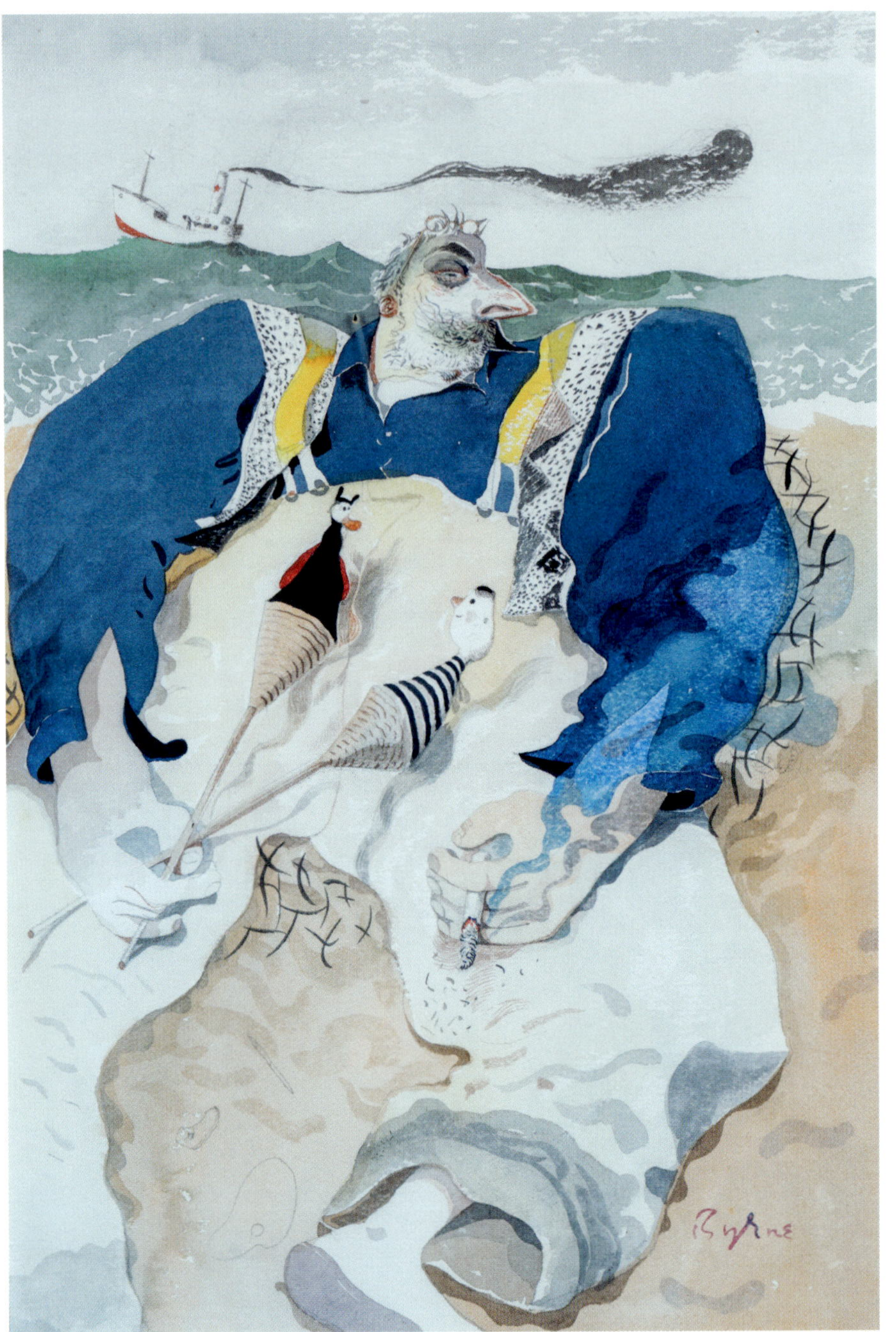

Two Pokey Hats on the Beach, 1997
Watercolour and ink on paper
80cm × 60cm
Private Collection

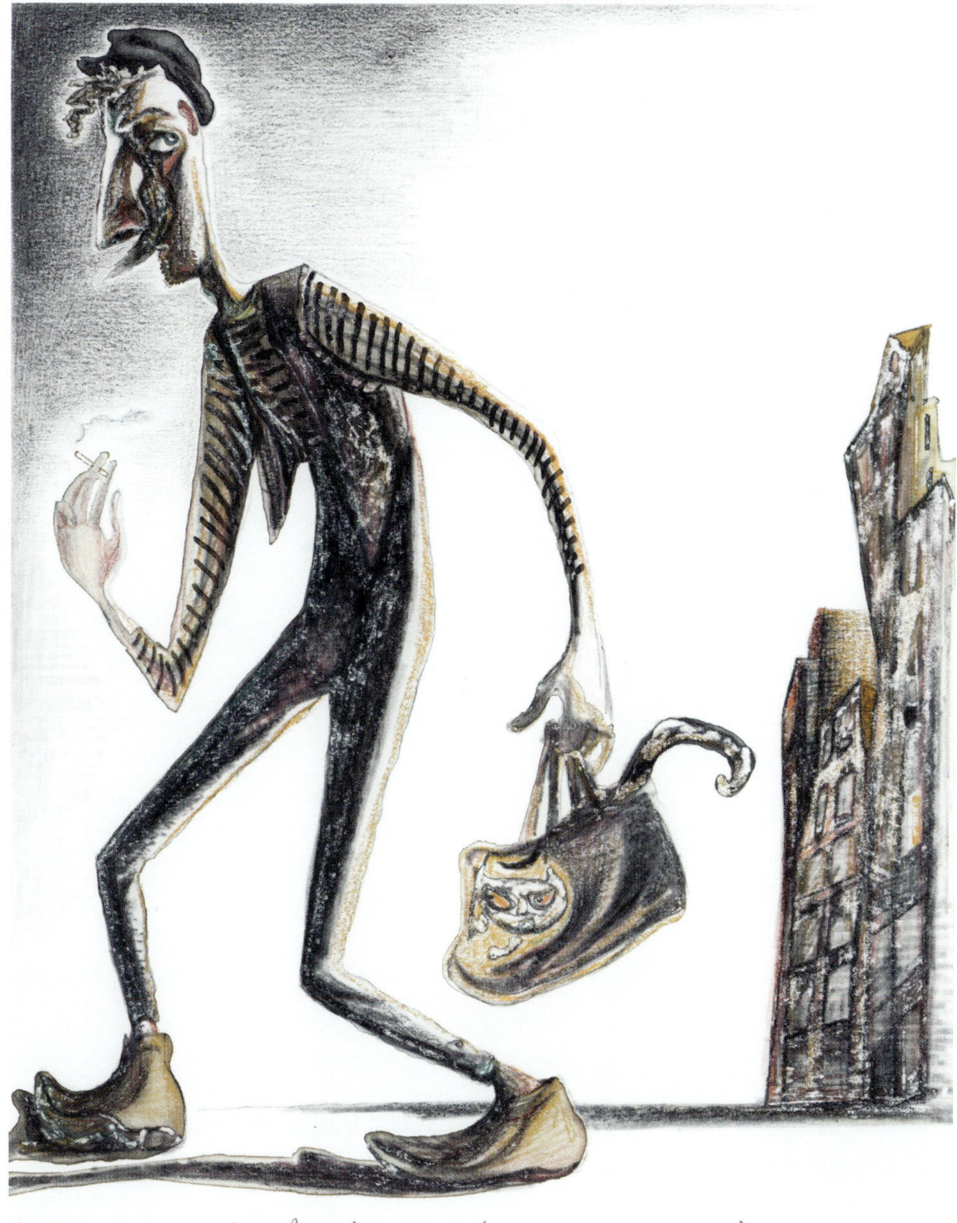

Cat Burglar, 2017
Watercolour and ink on paper
63cm × 51cm
Private Collection

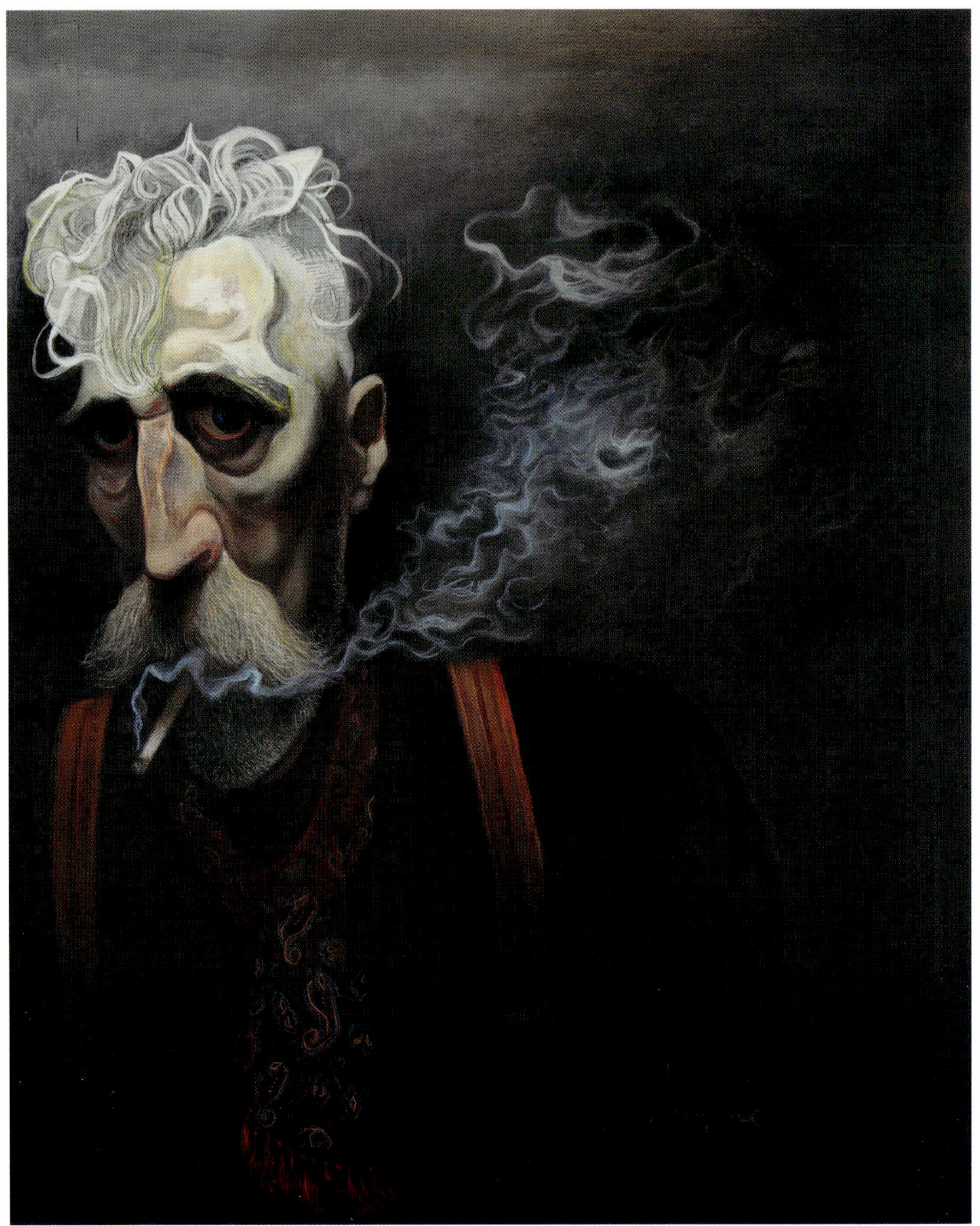

Big Selfie, 2014
Casein on paper
137cm × 112cm
Purchased in 2014 by the late
Angus Crichton-Miller

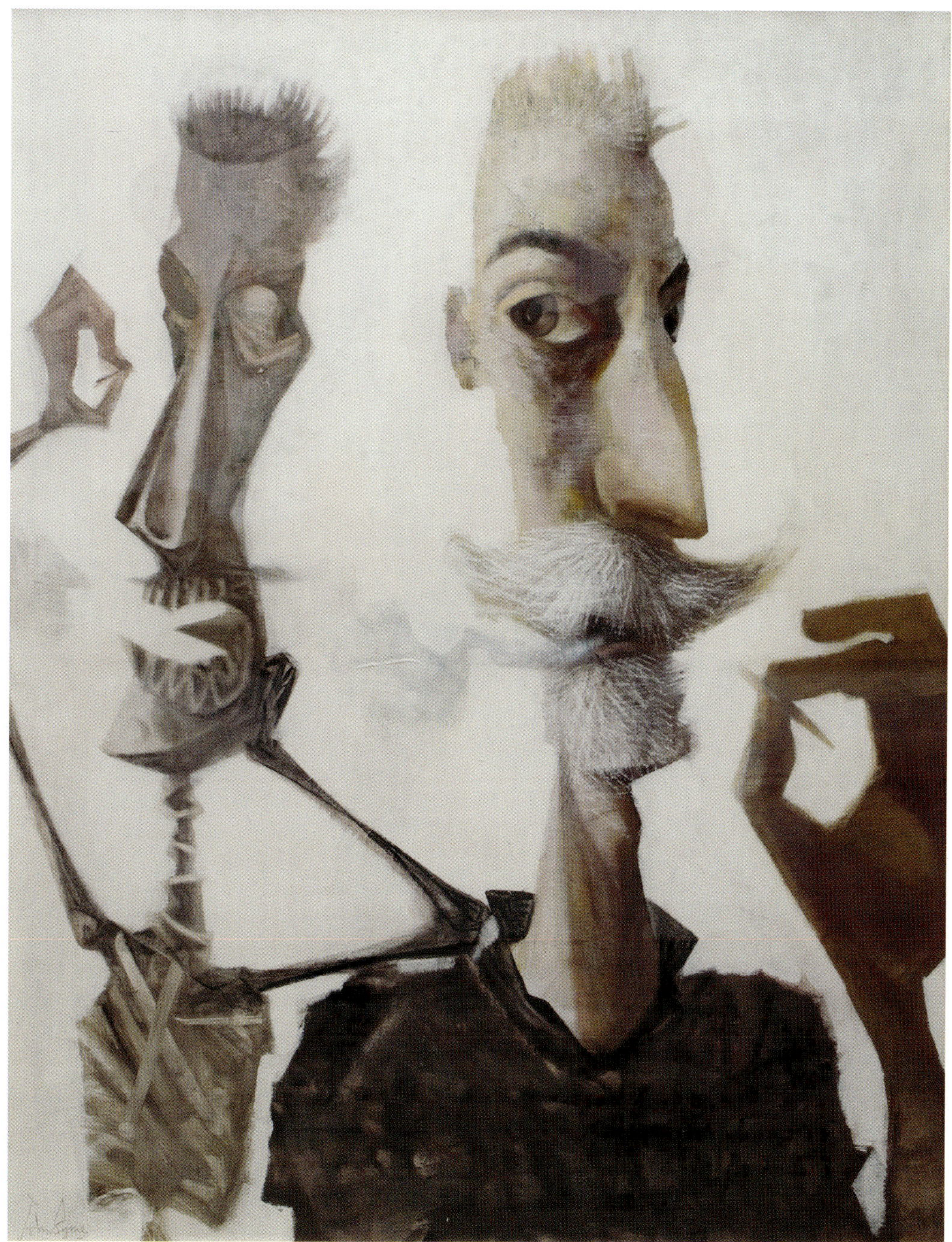

Me and My Shadow, 2006
Oil on board
145cm × 115cm
Private Collection

Portraits

Byrne moves between artistic styles, depending on how he views the sitter. His portraits are usually painted in a more realistic way than those, for example, done as Patrick, keeping the sitter recognizable.

He paints his friends and family members larger than life, with symbols of their work or passions woven into the paintings.

Mainly known for his paintings and prints, Byrne is also a very skilled draftsman as you can see in the studies in pencil and conté crayon on pp.82–83.

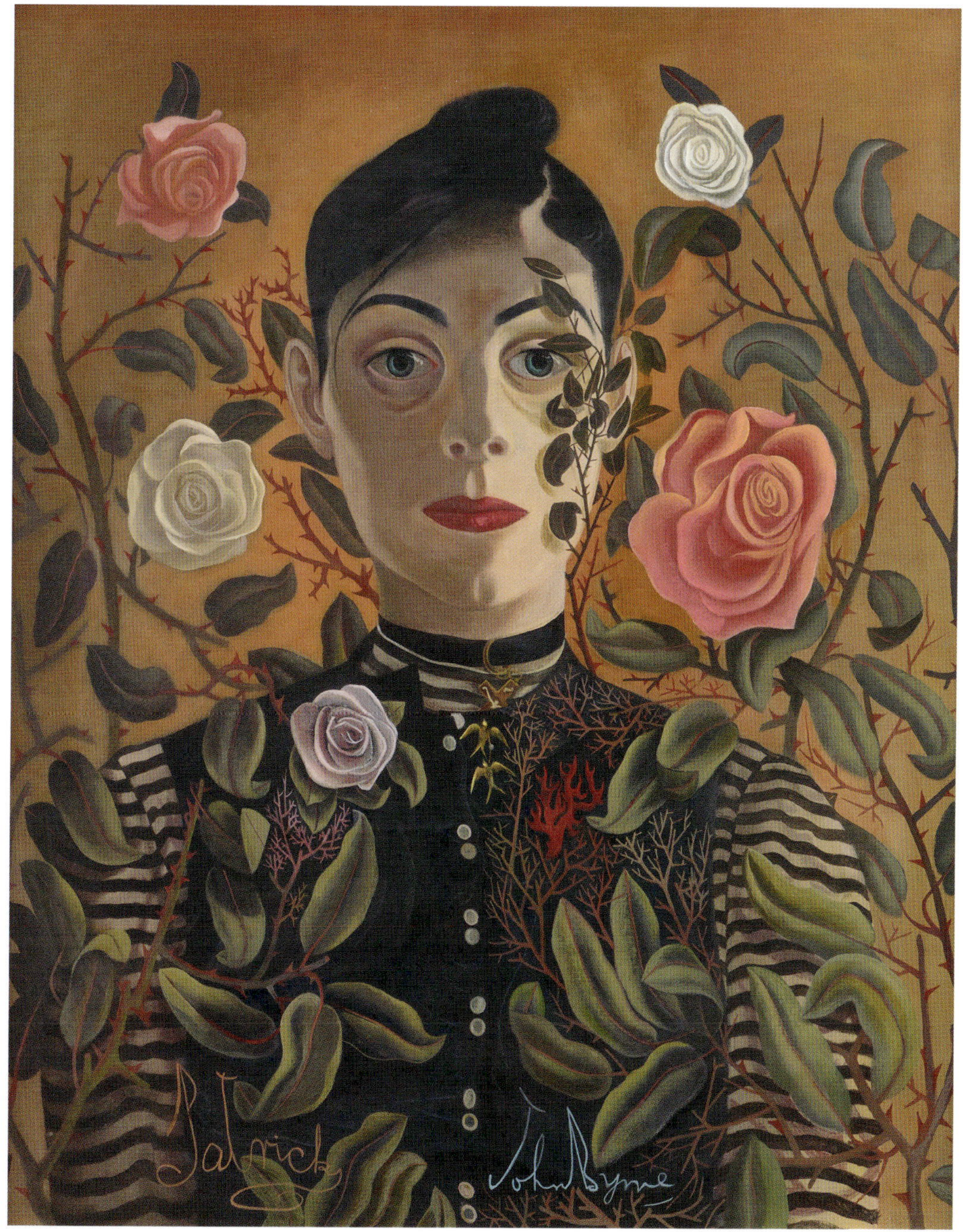

Jeanine with Flowers, 2011
Oil on canvas
83cm × 78cm
Lent by the artist

Byrne's wife Jeanine is an accomplished lighting designer, writer, creative and Pilates instructor. She adapted Byrne's children's book *Donald and Benoit* for the stage with the Pitlochry Festival Theatre.

Billy Connolly, Entertainer, 2002
Oil on canvas
74.9cm × 69.7cm
Lent by National Galleries Scotland
Purchased 2002
PG 3323

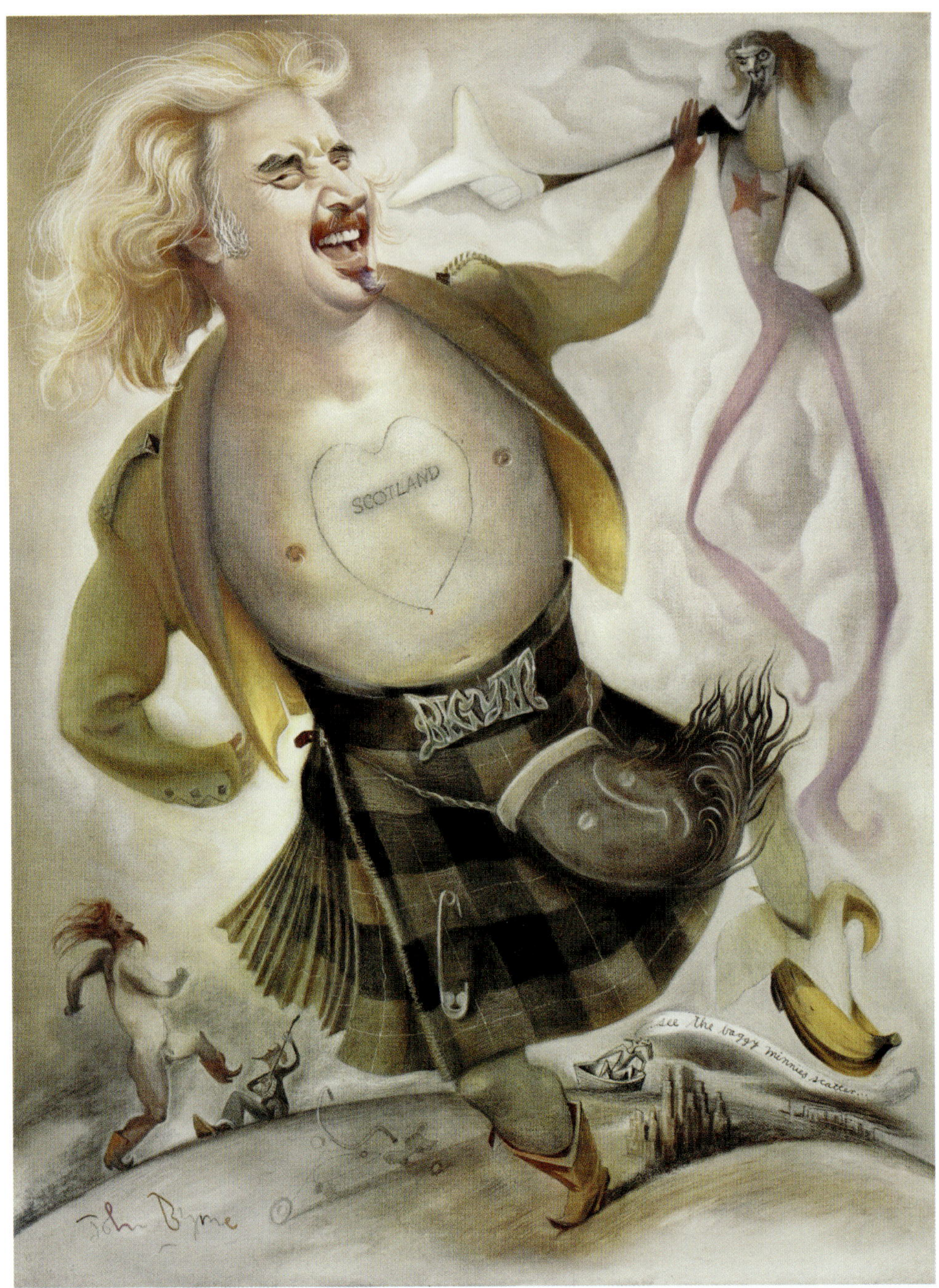

Painted for Connolly's sixtieth birthday, this shows multiple Connollys from various points in his career. There is a 1970s' spandex-clad Connolly, and the naked Connolly next to his motorbike from his *Around the World...*' TV series. The central 'Entertainer' has one foot in the past with his famous banana boots and the other near what looks like New York, where Connolly lived at the time.

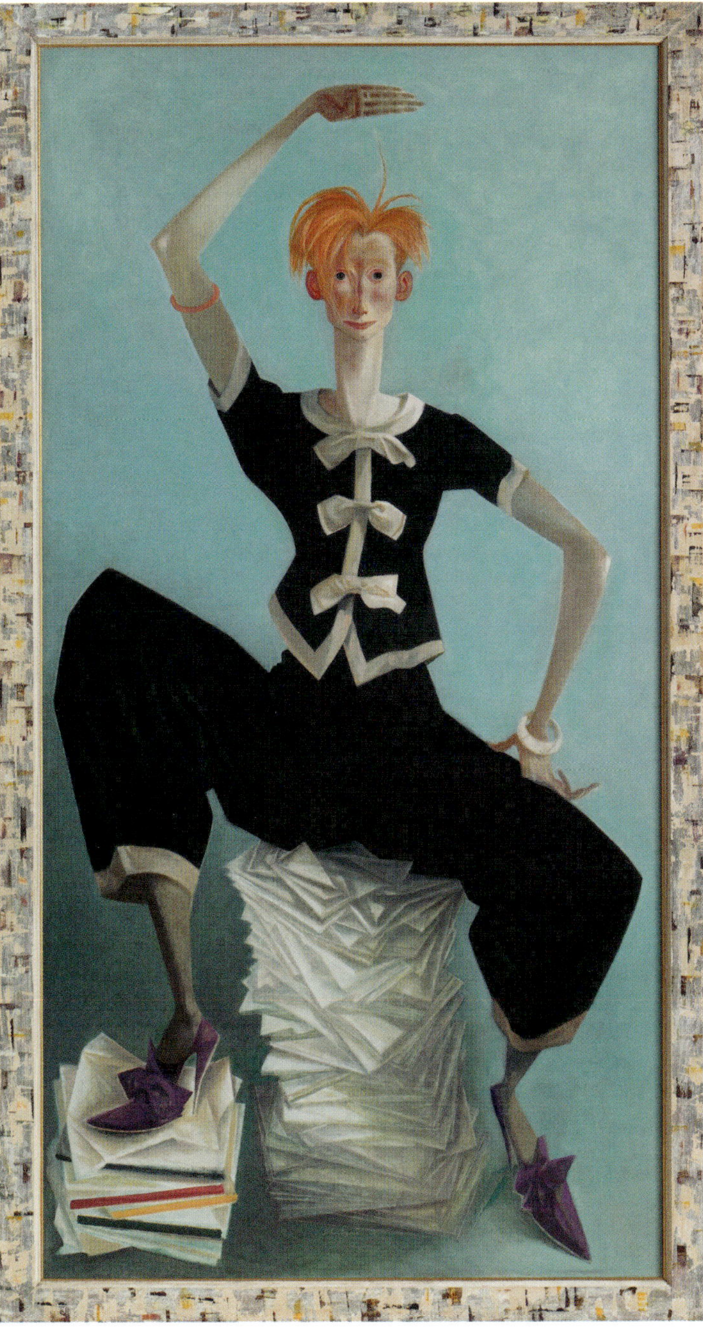

Red and Unread, 2002–04
Oil on board, frame painted by Byrne
262cm × 139cm
Andrew and Fiona Paterson/National
Galleries of Scotland. Long Loan In.
PGL 2512

This is a portrait of actor Tilda Swinton
sitting on a stack of scripts, some
read, some unread, the title a pun on
Swinton's red hair.

Portrait of John and Celie, 1985
Oil on canvas
154cm × 104cm
University of Dundee Museums

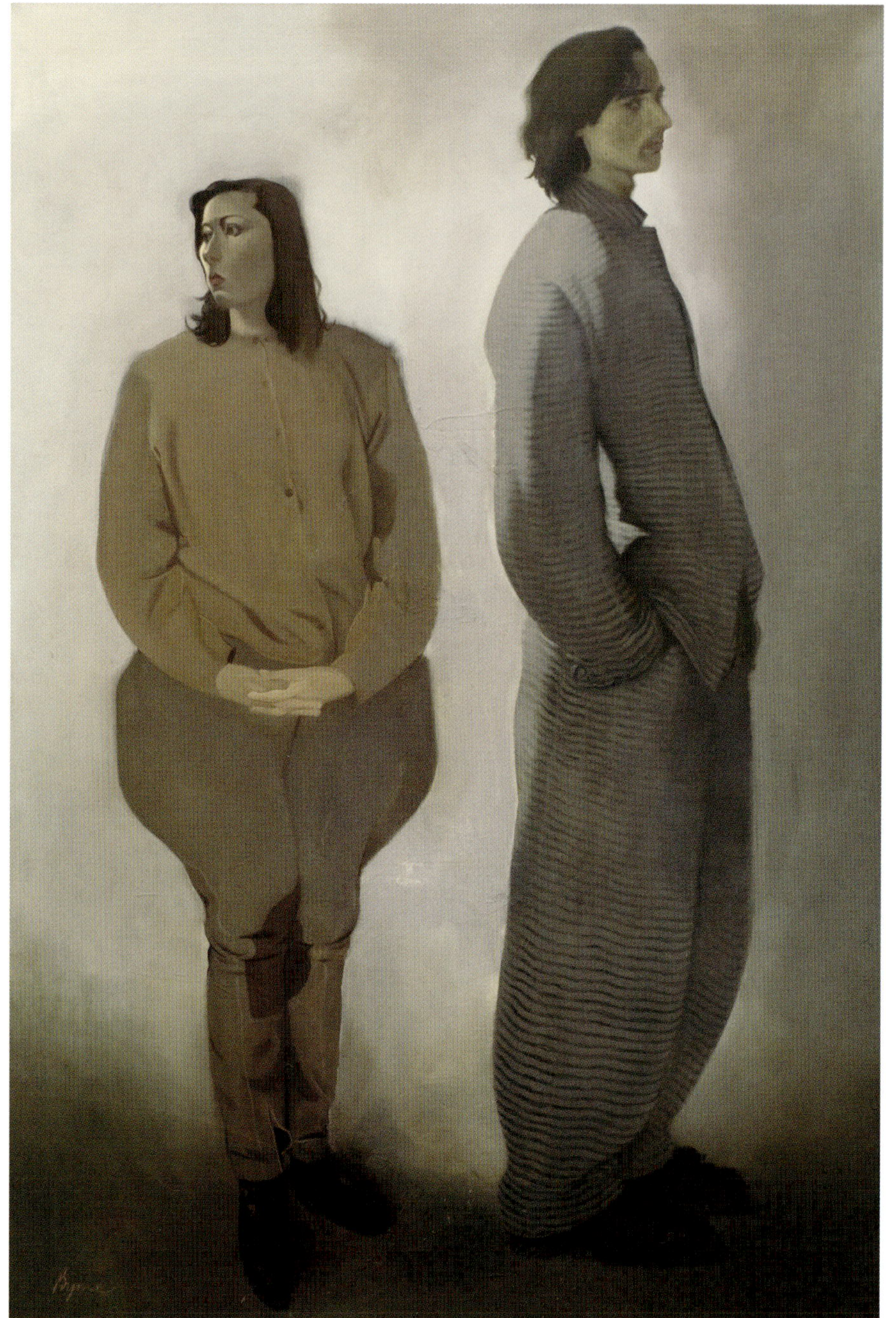

This painting is of Byrne's two older children, John and Celie.

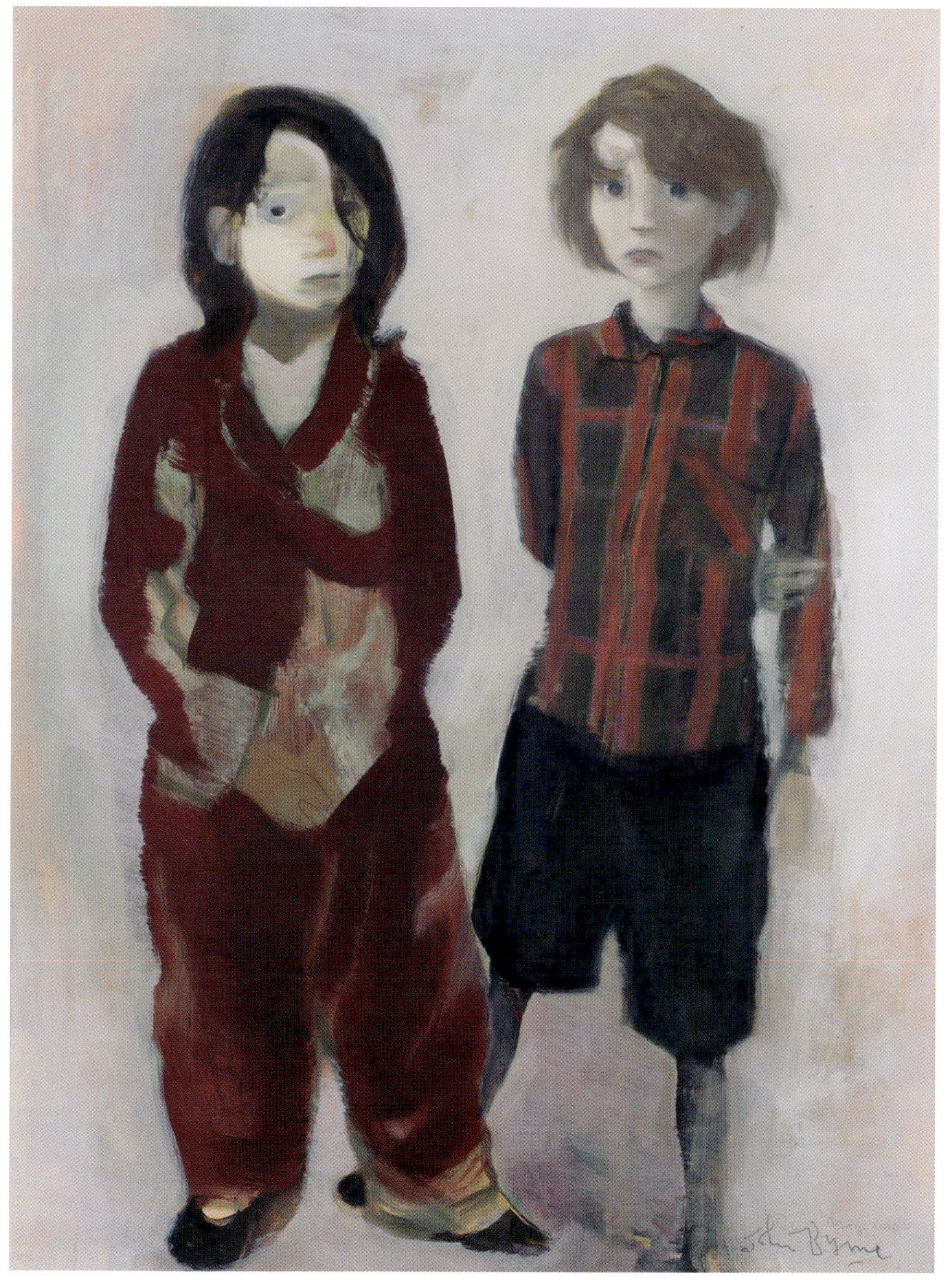

Self-reflection, 2001
Oil on board
143cm × 110cm
Private Collection

This painting is of Byrne's two younger children, twins Xavier and Honor.

Rebecca, 2010
Conté crayon on board
71.5cm × 56cm
Lent by the artist

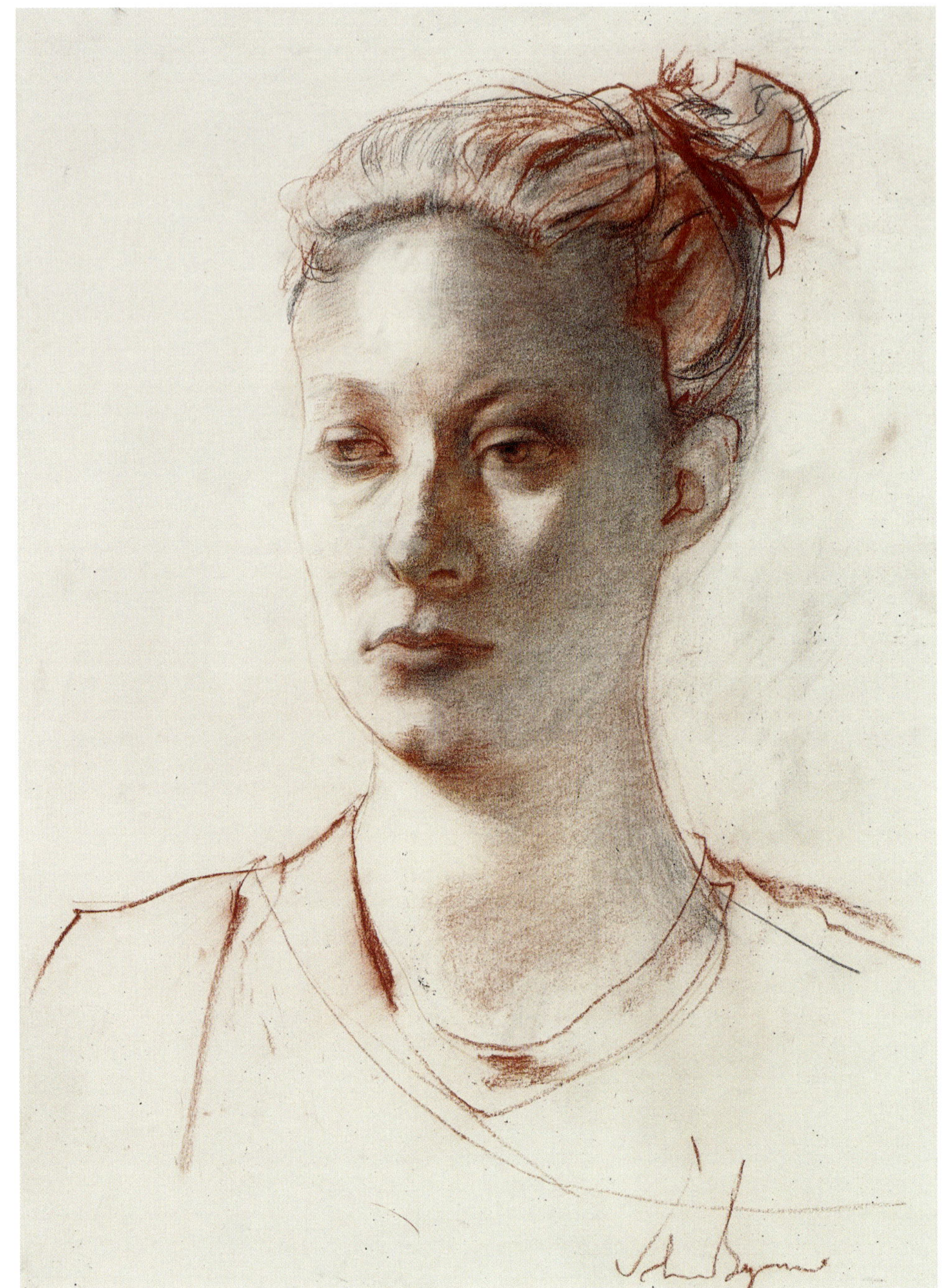

Rebecca is Byrne's stepdaughter.

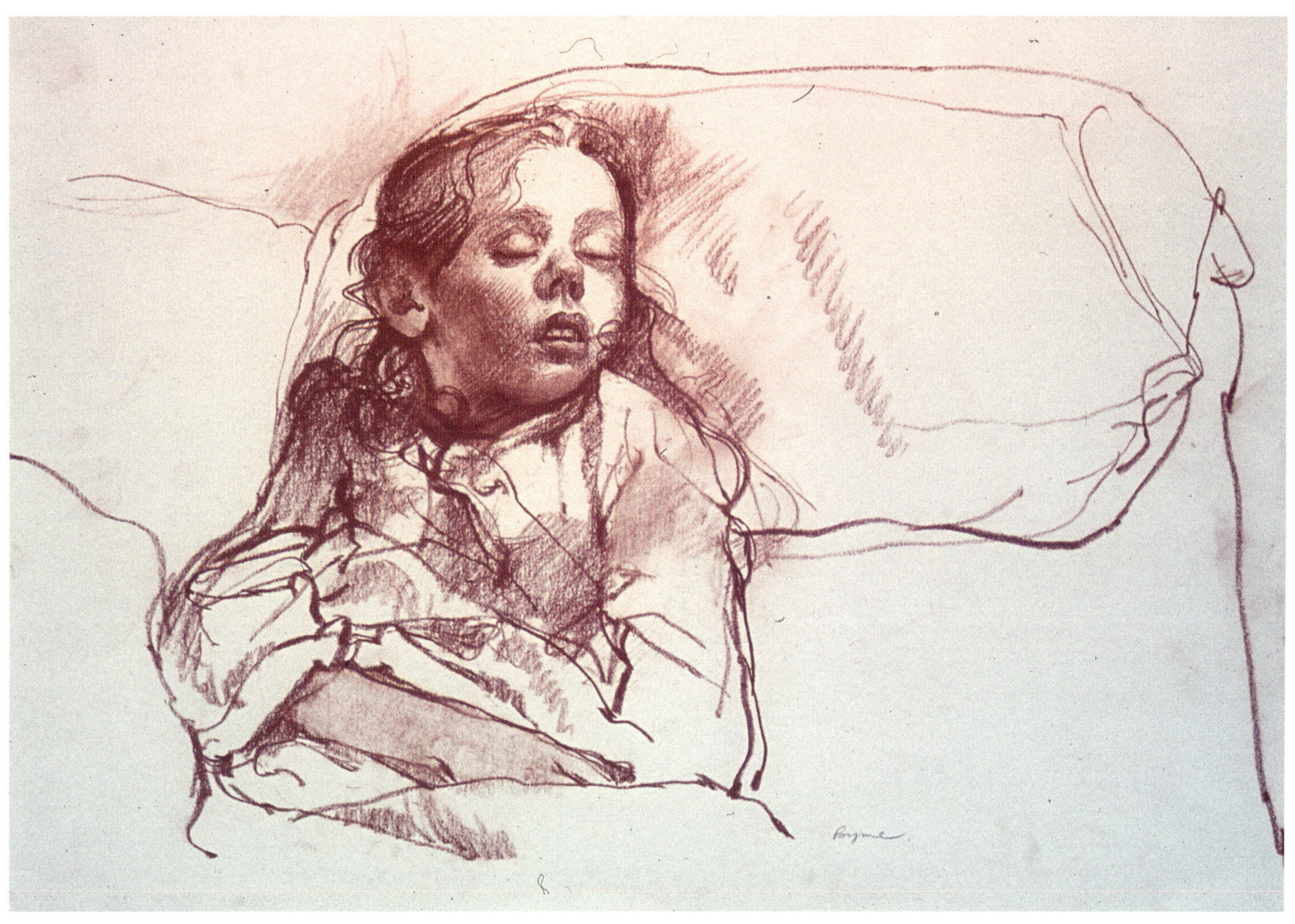

Celie Asleep, 1973
Conté on paper
54cm × 65.4cm
Lent by the City Art Centre, Museum and Galleries Edinburgh

A study of Byrne's daughter Celie. This wonderful drawing shows the skill that underpins all his artwork.

The many styles of Byrne

Byrne is able to turn his hand to anything, from stage designs to album covers. This section showcases even more of his diverse artistic style and subject matter, including examples from his substantial body of work in print, often working closely with Glasgow Print Studio. His paintings move between style and subjects, from Cubist harlequins, exquisite still-lifes, cherub-like 'Beach Boys', to darker, more narrative-driven paintings of dark woods or distressing scenes. But he can also produce delicate, finely crafted illustrations and small paintings on scraper board in mixed media. We can only give a very small sense of Byrne's vast practice and artistic skills.

Byrne's art school tutors said he could paint like the best artists in the world. He uses his natural skills to great effect, making any style his own, and proving he is one of the most gifted artists of the last 70 years.

Beach Boy with Fish Bone and Hat,
about 2009
Oil and acrylic on canvas
88.2cm × 103.3cm
Private Collection

The detail and brush work in this picture are outstanding. Look at the subtlety, you barely see the fish bone until on closer inspection you realize the skeleton on the boy's arm is actually a shadow.

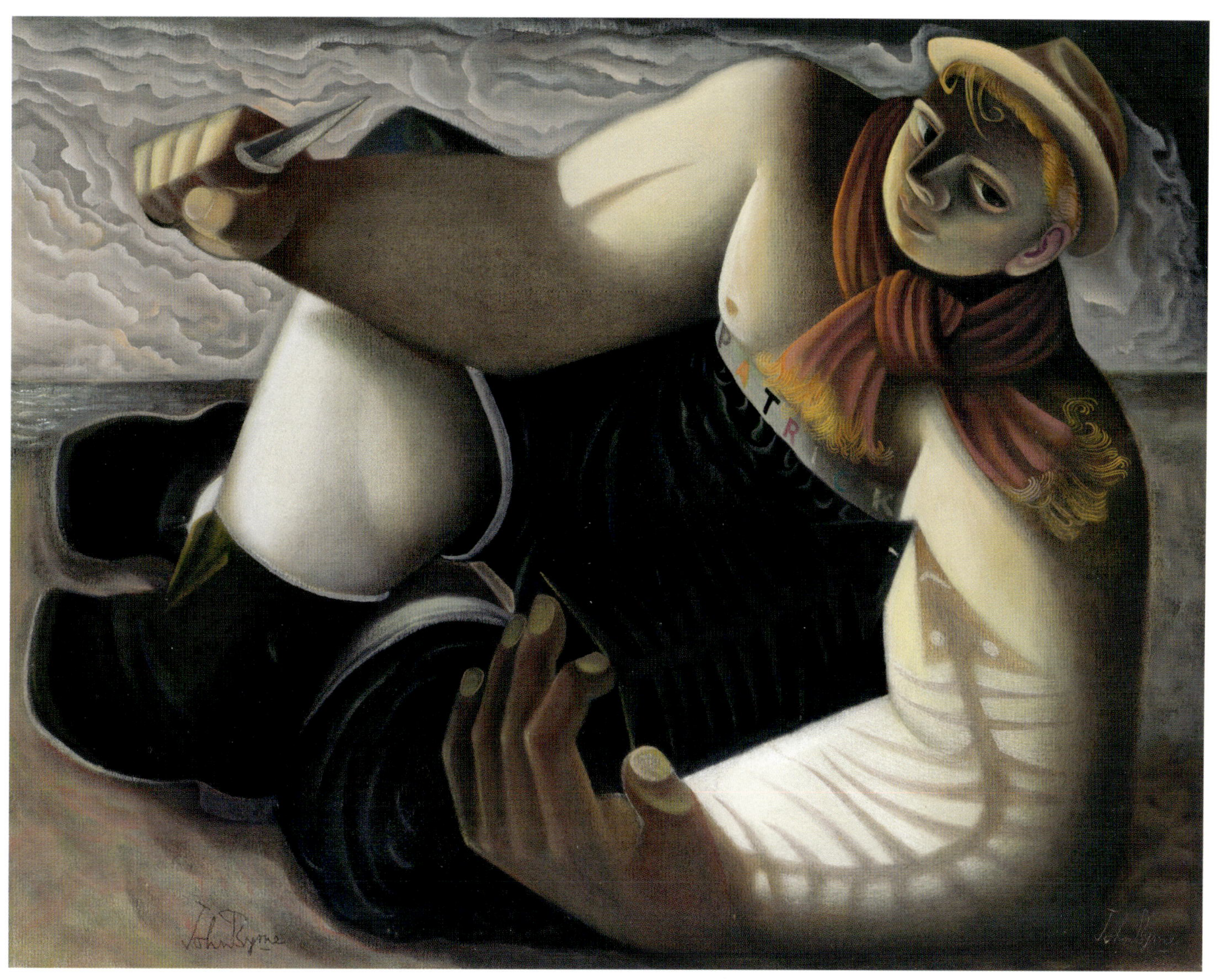

In Garden with Owl, about 2014
Oil on board
38cm × 31cm
Private Collection, Charles Marks

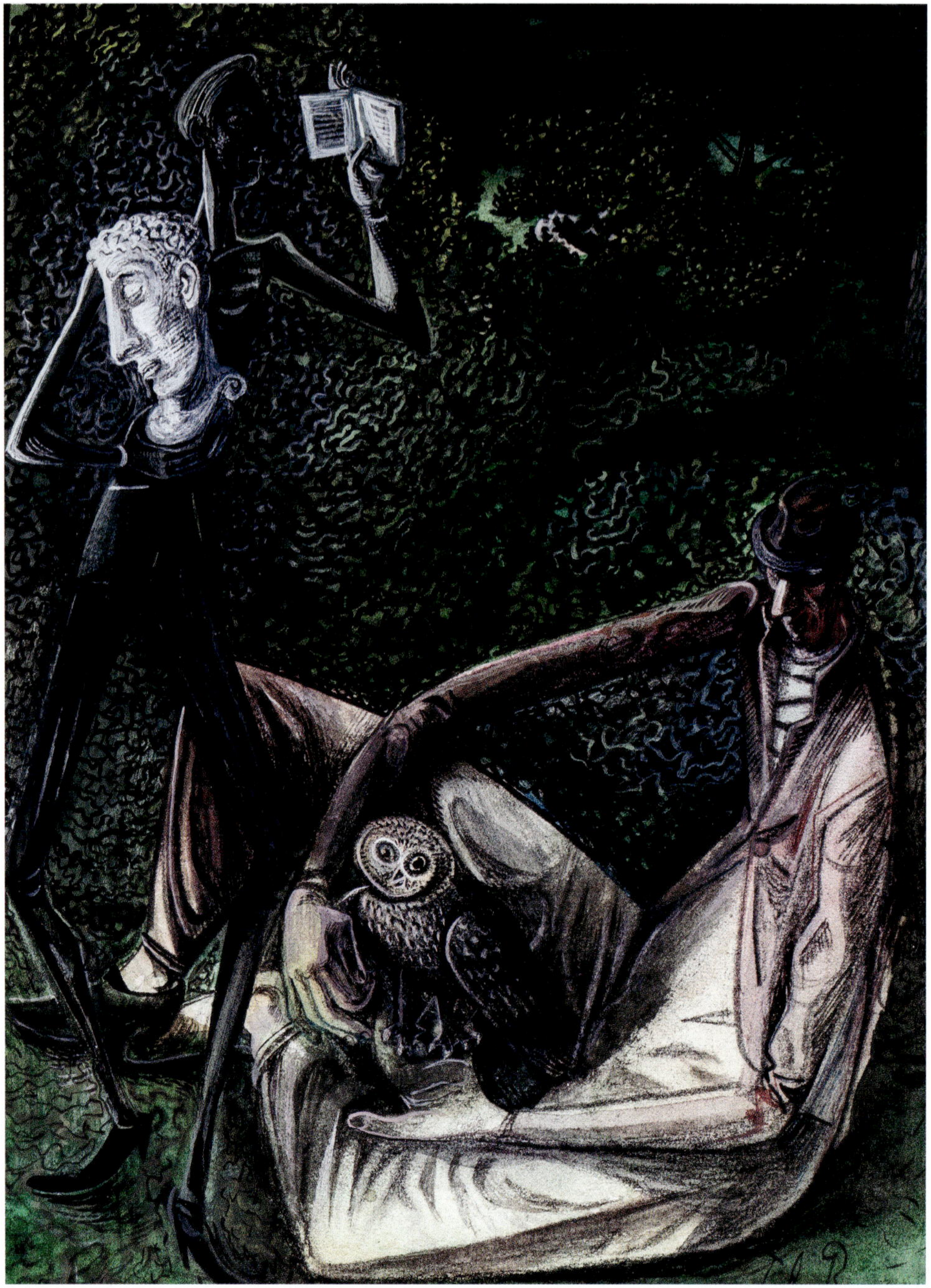

opposite:
North East Apocalypse, 2008
Oil on board
102cm × 108cm
Private Collection, Charles Marks

Based on drawings done in Orkney,
this dark but captivating painting
could be viewed as an expression
of inner turmoil.

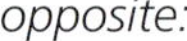

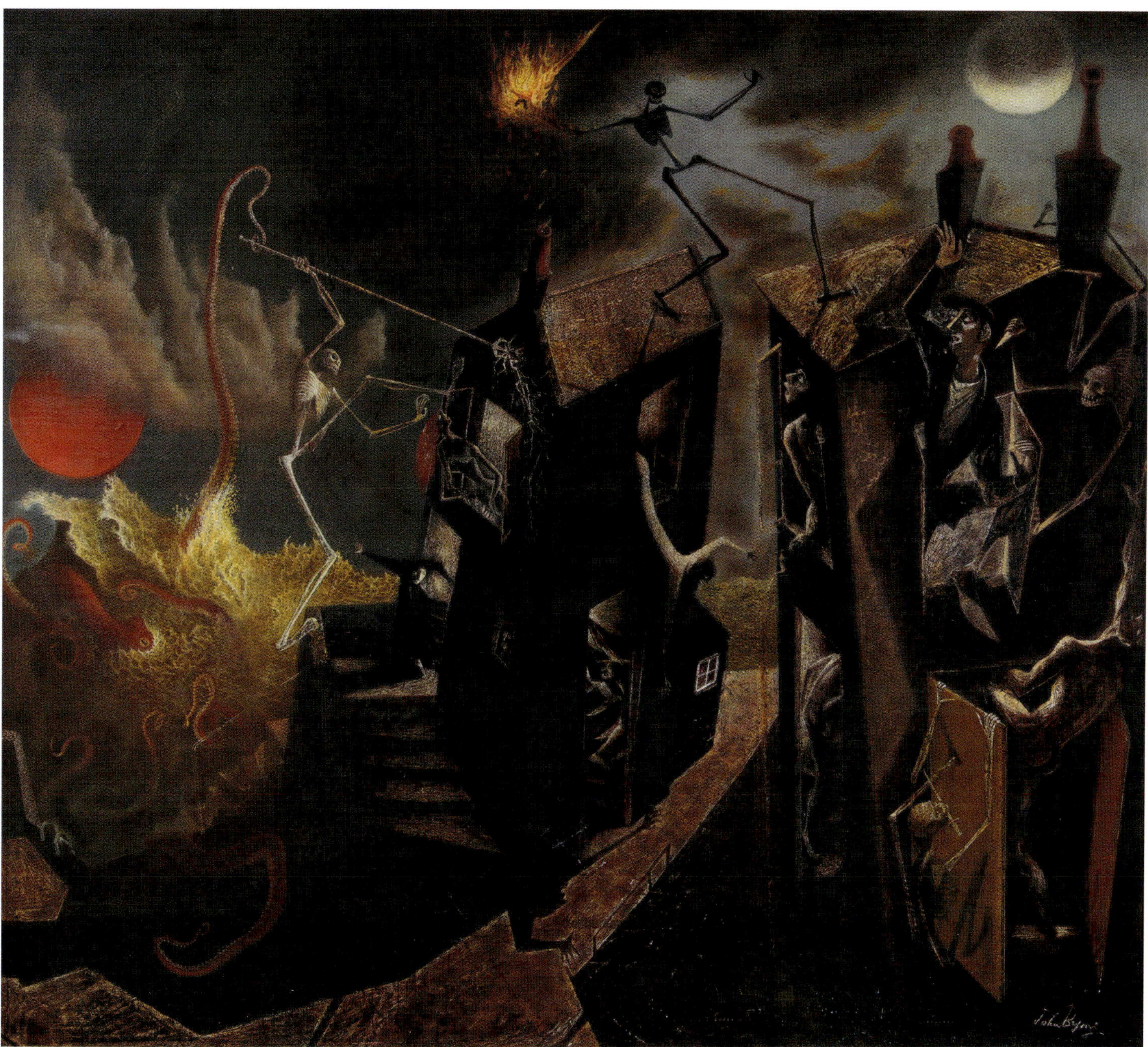

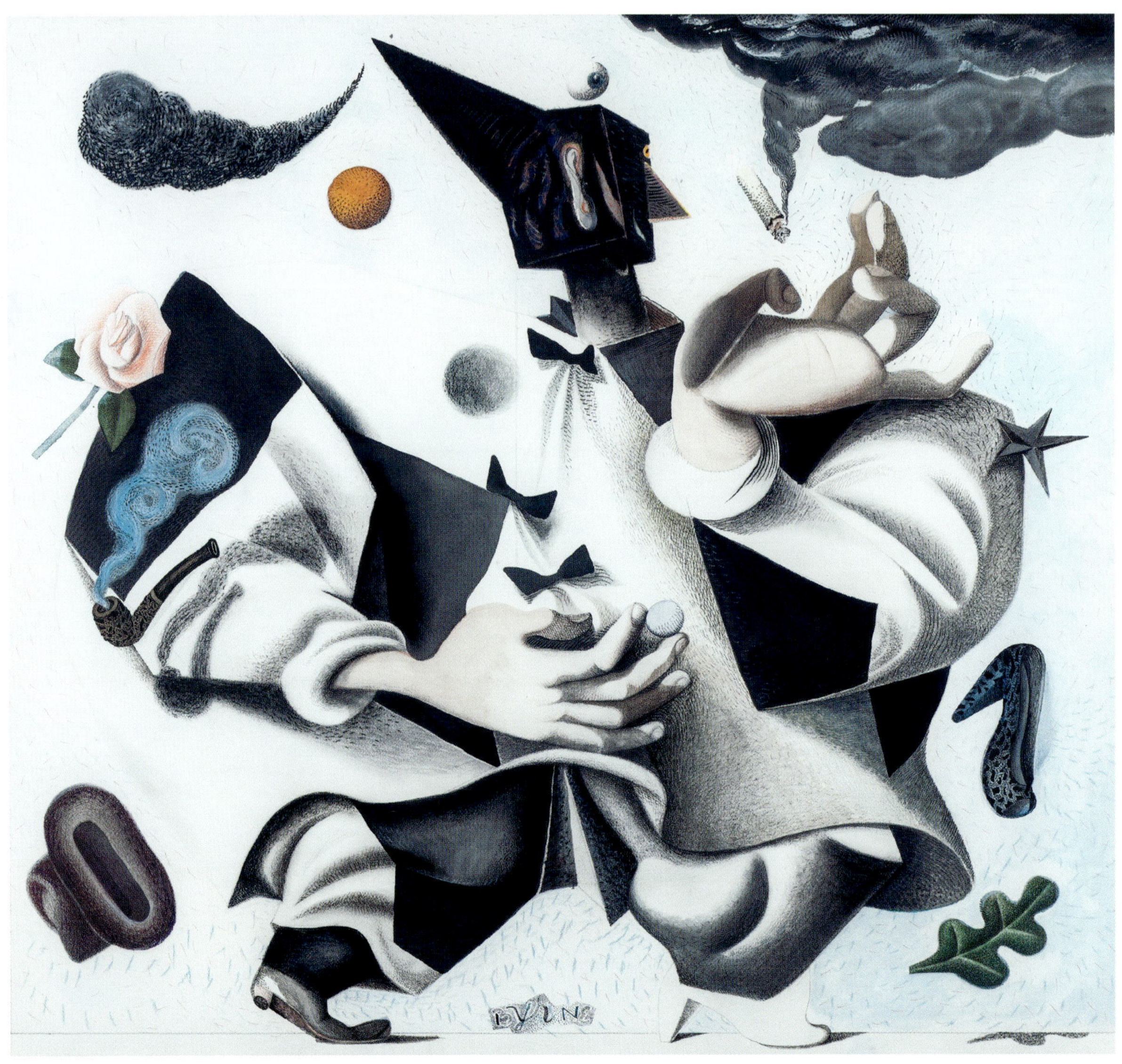

Pierrot, 2002
Paint on board
132cm × 137cm
Private Collection

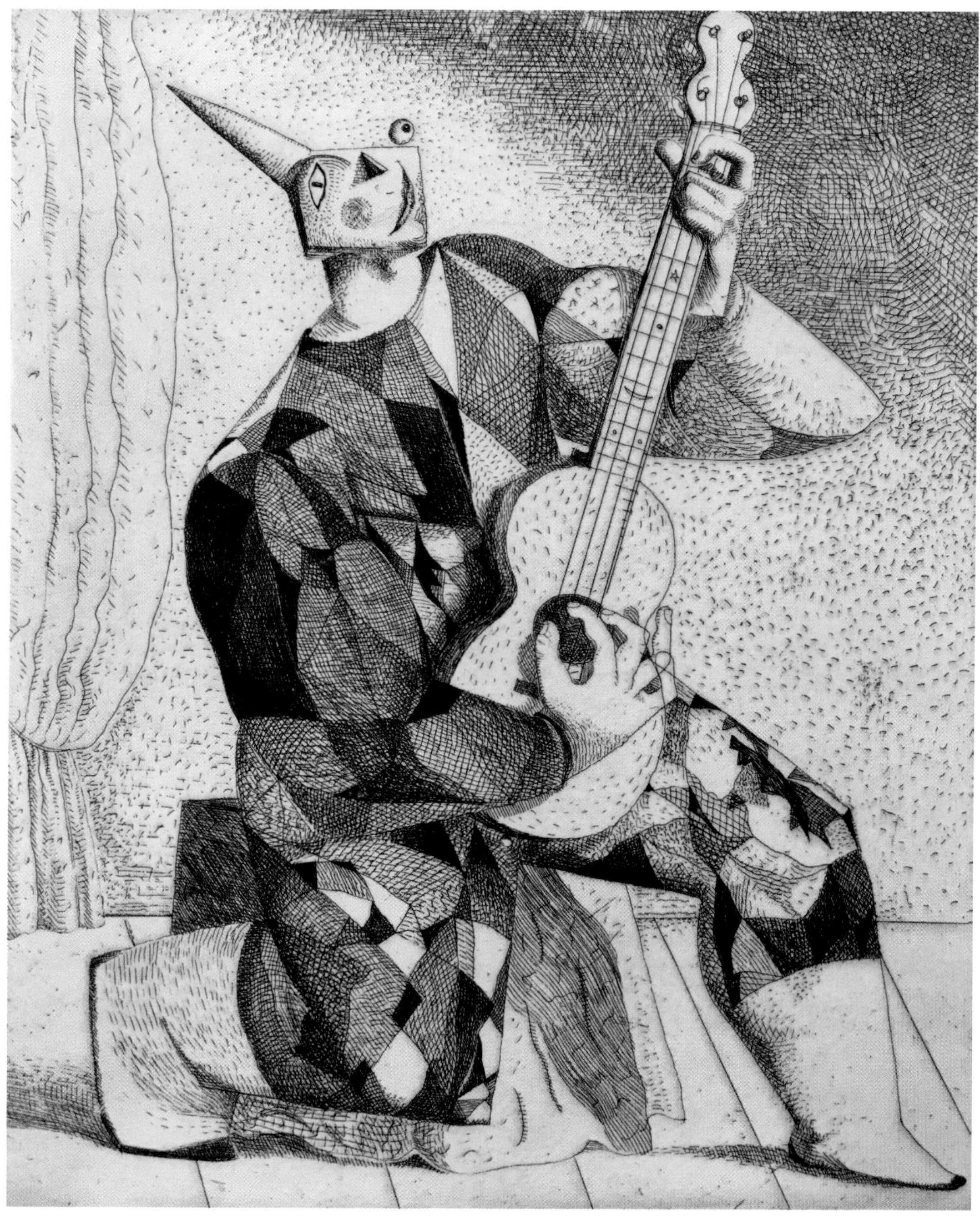

Harlequin with Guitar,
1998
Etching
64cm × 48cm
Lent by Glasgow Print Studio

Byrne has worked with
Glasgow Print Studio for
over 40 years. Working with
their Master Printers, he has
created an astonishingly
varied body of printed works.

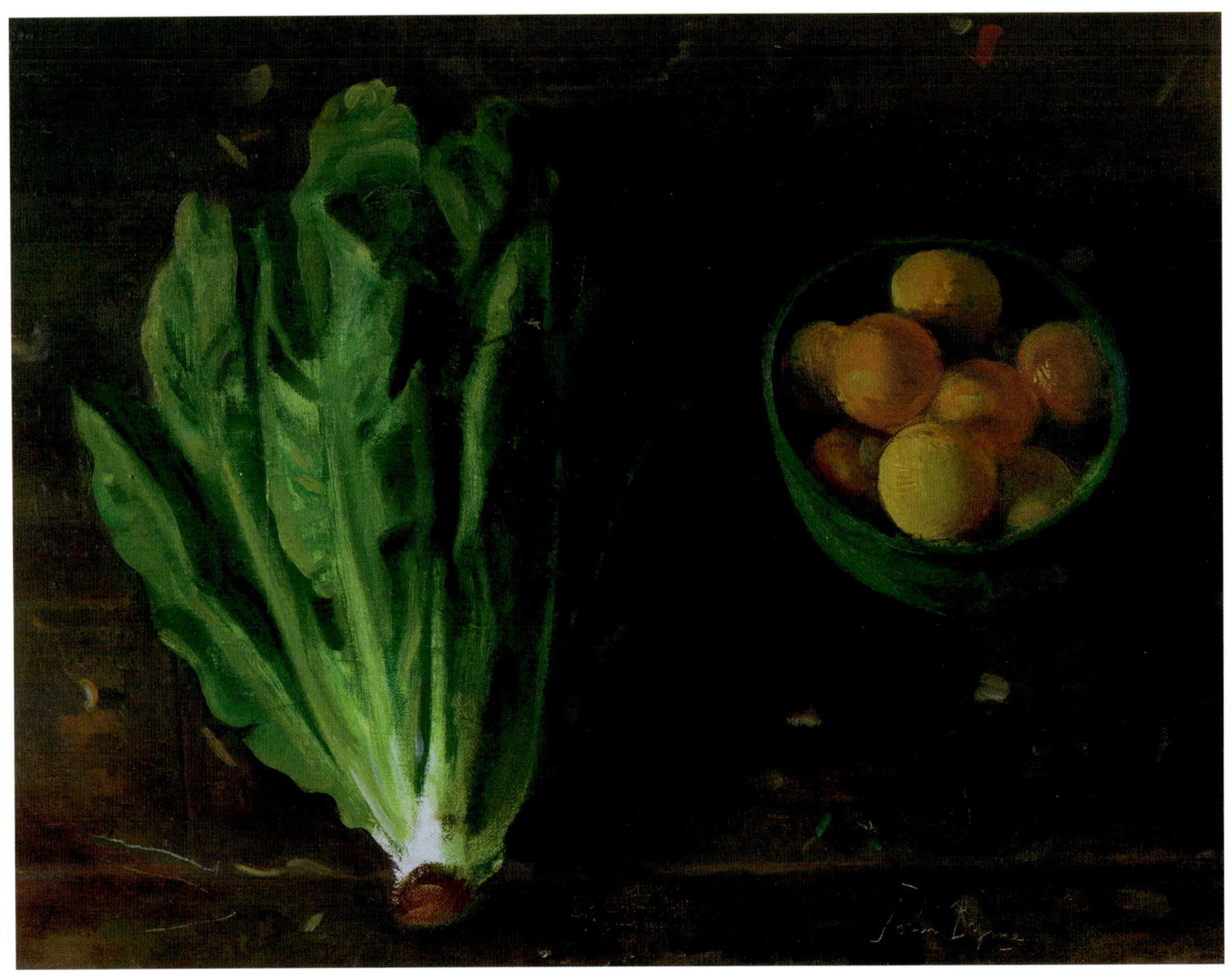

Lettuce and Prunes, about 2015
Oil on canvas, 67cm × 77cm
Private Collection, Charles Marks

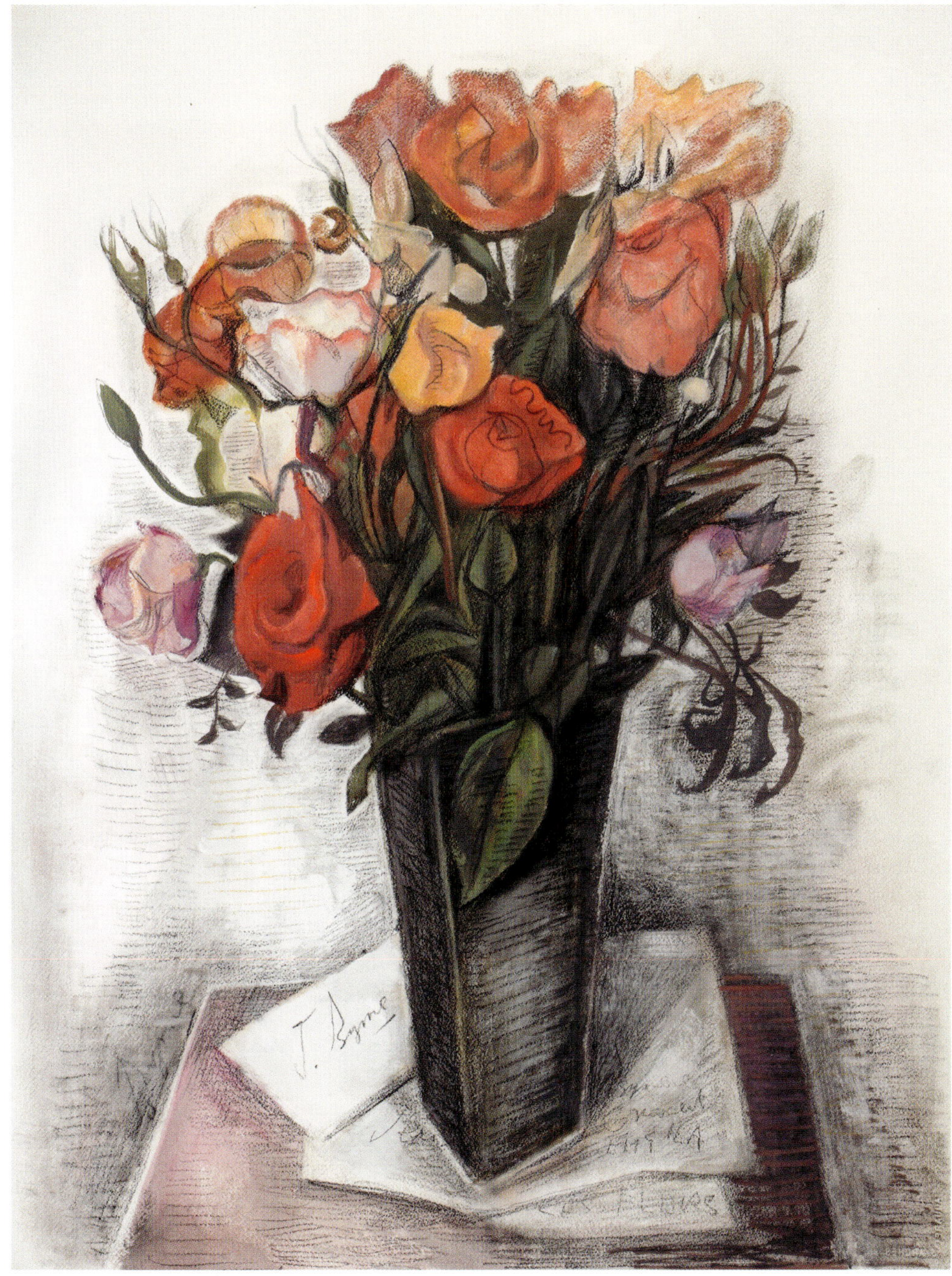

Say it with Flowers, 2015
Watercolour, graphite, on paper
86cm × 64cm
Private Collection, Charles Marks

Chronology

Reproduced courtesy of The Fine Art Society

1940 Born in Paisley, second son of Patrick Byrne and Alice, née McShane

1957 Leaves school without taking Highers (examinations), gets job as 'slab boy' in local carpet factory AF Stoddard & Co.

1958 Fails first year exams at The Glasgow School of Art and has to resit

1961 Transfers to Edinburgh School of Art for one year

1962 Returns to The Glasgow School of Art

1963 Graduates with Diploma in Drawing and Painting, wins Newbery Medal, Hutchison Prize for Drawing, awarded Bellahouston Scholarship to travel to Perugia

1964 Marries, and son John Francis is born. Lives in Renfrew and becomes graphic designer for Scottish TV

1965 Daughter Celie born; exhibition at 208 Gallery, Glasgow; exhibition at Crestine Gallery, Edinburgh

1966 Leaves Scottish TV, joins AF Stoddard as a carpet designer

1967 Correspondence with Magritte, adopts Patrick as an alter ego; first exhibition at Portal Gallery, London: *Patrick Byrne: Portal's Paisley Primitive Painter* (December)

1968 Leaves AF Stoddard & Co, becomes a full-time painter; *Patrick at Portal*, Portal Gallery, London (Nov–Dec)

1969 *Patrick at Portal*, Portal Gallery, London (December)

1971 Travels with family to Los Angeles to work on animated film with Donovan Leitch, *An Old-Fashioned Picture Book;* exhibition at Rex Irwin Gallery, Sydney; *Nine Large Patrick Paintings*, Portal Gallery, London (December)

1972 Designs set for *The Great Northern Welly Boot Show*, King's Theatre, Glasgow; *Patrick at Portal: an exhibition of New Smaller Paintings*, Portal Gallery, London (October)

1973 Designs set for *The Cheviot, the Stag and the Black, Black Oil* for 7:84 Scotland; Aitken Dott Gallery, Edinburgh

1974 Paints gable-end mural *Boy on Dogback*, Crawford Street, Glasgow

1975 Exhibition at Clunes Gallery, Sydney; *John Byrne: Paintings and Drawings*, Third Eye Centre, Glasgow; Paisley Museum and Art Galleries; Aberdeen Gallery; withdraws from exhibiting publicly until 1991

1976 Radio version of *Writer's Cramp*, BBC Scotland

1977 Stage version of *Writer's Cramp*, Edinburgh Fringe, transferring to Bush Theatre, London and Mickery Theatre, Amsterdam

1978 *The Slab Boys*, The Traverse Theatre, Edinburgh, transferring to Royal Court, London, winning *Evening Standard* award for most promising playwright

1979 *Normal Service*, Hampstead Theatre Club, London; *The Loveliest Night of the Year* (later called *Cuttin' a Rug*), The Traverse Theatre, Edinburgh; becomes Writer-in-Residence, Borderline Theatre Co. Writes, directs and designs *Dick Whittington* for Borderline; writes *Cara Coco* for Radio Scotland

1980 *Hooray for Hollywood*, Louisville, Kentucky; becomes Writer-in-Residence, Duncan of Jordanstone School of Art, Dundee

1982 *Still Life*, The Traverse Theatre, Edinburgh

1983 *The Slab Boys*, The Playhouse Theatre, New York

1984 Writes episode of *Crown Court;* becomes Associate Director and designer at Leicester Haymarket Theatre

1985 Adaption of *The London Cuckolds* opens at Leicester Haymarket Theatre; designs Peter Arnott's *White Rose* at The Traverse Theatre, Edinburgh; writes *Tutti Frutti*

1987 *Tutti Frutti* transmitted on BBC

1988 BBC2 transmits *Byrne about Byrne*, written and directed by Byrne for BBC *Arena*

1990 *Your Cheatin' Heart* is transmitted on BBC1 with Tilda Swinton as Cissie Crouch

1991 Returns to exhibiting and begins an intense period of work at Glasgow Print Studio; *Your Cheatin' Heart*, William Hardie Gallery, Glasgow; *Patrick's Day,* Portal Gallery, London (June); *Hankies,* William Hardie Gallery, Glasgow

1992 Moves to London; *Colquhoun and MacBryde*, Royal Court, London

1993 BBC2 transmits Boswell and Johnson's *Tour of the Western Isles*, written and directed by Byrne

1994 *La Terre Sauvage*, Glasgow Print Studio

1995 *New Works*, The Scottish Gallery, Edinburgh

1996 Directs film version of *The Slab Boys* in a Glasgow warehouse

1997 *The Slab Boys* premiers at Edinburgh Film Festival; Byrne and Tilda Swinton have twins, Xavier and Honor; adaptation of *The Government Inspector*, Almeida, London; House for an Art Lover, Glasgow; *The Slab Boys*, The Scottish Gallery, Edinburgh; *John Byrne Paintings at Portal*, Portal Gallery, London (October–November)

1998 Settles in Tain; *The Slab Boys Movie Exhibition*, Duncan R Miller Fine Arts, Glasgow

1999 *New Editions*, Glasgow Print Studio; *Flotsam and Jetsam*, Art.TM Gallery, Inverness

2000 Post Office issues Byrne-designed 20-pence millennium stamp; *Byrne@60: The Unsolved Artist*, Paisley Museum and Galleries

2001 Awarded an MBE for services to literature and theatre (Byrne later returned it in protest against the war against Iraq); two self portraits included in *Four Hundred Years of Scottish Portraits 1600-2000* at Bourne Fine Art, Edinburgh

2002 *Recent Works*, Glasgow Print Studio

2003 Writes musical *Underwood Lane; Six Portraits of Scots Politicians*, The National Portrait Gallery, Edinburgh

2004 An adaptation of Chekhov's *Uncle Varick* opens at The Royal Lyceum, Edinburgh; *New Work*, The Fine Art Society, London; *A Life in Small Pictures*, The Fine Art Society, Edinburgh

2005 *Dead and Alive*, The Fine Art Society, London

2006 A stage version of *Tutti Frutti* for the National Theatre of Scotland opens at His Majesty's Theatre, Aberdeen; *Small Works – Portraits and Still Life*, The Scottish Gallery, Edinburgh; *Me and Them – Self Portraits and Character Studies*, The Fine Art Society, Edinburgh; awarded an Honorary Doctorate from Gray's School of Art, Aberdeen

2007 Becomes a full member at the Royal Scottish Academy

2008 *Nova Scotia*, The Traverse Theatre, Edinburgh; *John Byrne*, Moray Art Centre; *Prints & Works on Paper*, The Fine Art Society, Edinburgh

2009 *Cornerboys and Angels*, Glasgow Print Studio; *John Byrne: prints*, The Fine Art Society, Edinburgh

2010 New version of Chekhov's *The Cherry Orchard*, Royal Lyceum, Edinburgh

2011 *Moonlight and Music*, The Open Eye Gallery, Edinburgh; *Boogie-Woogie*, The Rendezvous Gallery, Aberdeen; awarded an Honorary Doctorate from the University of Dundee; *Donald and Benoit* written and illustrated by John Byrne (published by Rizzoli)

2012 *The Joyful Mysteries*, The Fine Art Society, London

2013 A new mural is completed in the dome at The King's Theatre, Edinburgh; *Bad Smoky Joe and The Dark Wildwoods*, The Rendezvous Gallery, Aberdeen

2014 *Dead End*, The Fine Art Society, Edinburgh; *Sitting Ducks*, Scottish National Portrait Gallery; a new adaption of *Uncle Varick* opens at The Royal Lyceum, Edinburgh; marries Jeanine Davies; a new adaptation of *Three Sisters* opens at Tron Theatre, Glasgow

2015 *A Matter of Life and Death*, The Fine Art Society, London; *Zoo at the End of My Brush*, Brown Gallery, Tain; new production of *The Slab Boys* opens at the Citizens Theatre, Glasgow and King's Theatre, Edinburgh

2016 *Moonshine*, The Fine Art Society, Edinburgh

2017 *Don't Fence Me In*, The Rendezvous Gallery, Aberdeen; *Lullaby of Broadway*, The Fine Art Society, London; *Rock 'N' Roll*, The Fine Art Society, Edinburgh; paints portrait of Billy Connolly for BBC1 documentary *Billy Connolly: Portrait of a Lifetime*; the portrait becomes a mural in Glasgow

2018 *The Boy and the Jabberwock: an exhibition of early works*, The Fine Art Society, Edinburgh; *John Byrne: Rogues' Gallery*, Royal Scottish Academy, Edinburgh; the set designs for *The Cheviot, the Stag and the Black, Black Oil for 7:84* (1973) go on display at the V&A Dundee, loaned by The National Library of Scotland; *Alasdair Gray and John Byrne: Two Great Glasgow Polymaths*, The Royal Glasgow Institute of the Fine Arts, Glasgow

2019 BBC Scotland re-broadcasts the six original episodes of *Tutti Frutti*; *John Byrne: Then Till Now*, The Fine Art Society, Edinburgh

2020 *John Byrne: Welcome to My World*, The Fine Art Society, Edinburgh

2021 *Tennis Elbow* audio drama (sequel to *Writer's Cramp*) broadcast on Sound Stage, Pitlochry Festival Theatre and Royal Lyceum Theatre, Edinburgh; *Donald and Benoit* adapted for the theatre as an audio drama by John's wife Jeanine Byrne and broadcast on Sound Stage, Pitlochry Festival Theatre

2022 *Ceci n'est pas une Rétrospective*, The Fine Art Society, Edinburgh; *John Byrne: A Big Adventure. Artist, Writer and Theatre Maker*, Kelvingrove Art Gallery and Museum, Glasgow; *Underwood Lane*, Johnstone Town Hall, and Tron Theatre, Glasgow

Works written by John Byrne

(From *John Byrne: Art and Life*, by Robert Hewison, published by Lund Humphries, reproduced by kind permission of the author.)

Works are listed under their established titles, beginning with date of first performance, followed by published versions and revivals in chronological order.

Babes in the Wood, Borderline at Citizens Theatre, Glasgow, 28 November 1980

Boswell and Johnson's Tour of the Western Isles, written and directed by Byrne, BBC2, October 1993

Byrne About Byrne, written and directed by Byrne, produced by Andy Park, BBC *Arena*, 1 April 1988

Candy Kisses, Bush Theatre, London, May 1984; Traverse, Edinburgh, November 1984

Cara Coco, radio play, BBC Scotland, 1979; Borderline Theatre, Ayr, 1981

The Cherry Orchard (after Chekhov), Lyceum Theatre, Edinburgh, 16 April 2010

Colquhoun and MacBryde, Royal Court, London, September 1992; published London: Faber & Faber, 1993; revived Paisley Arts Centre, March 1993; rewritten version Dundee Rep, March 2000

Cuttin' a Rug, first performed as *The Loveliest Night of the Year*, Traverse, Edinburgh, 19 May 1979; broadcast as *The Staffie*, BBC Radio Scotland, 1980; later revised as *Threads*, Hampstead

Theatre Club, London, March 1980; published as *Threads* in *A Decade's Drama: Six Scottish Plays* Todmorden: Woodhouse Books, 1980; revived as *Cuttin' a Rug*, part 2 of *Paisley Patterns: The Slab Boys Trilogy*, Traverse, Edinburgh, May 1982; published as *Cuttin' a Rug*, in *The Traverse Plays 3*, Edinburgh: Salamander Press

Donald and Benoit, New York: Universe Publishing (Rizzoli), 2011; adapted for the theatre as an audio drama by Jeanine Byrne and broadcast on Sound Stage, Pitlochry Festival Theatre, 2021

The Government Inspector (after Gogol), Almeida Theatre, London, 4 December 1997; published by Oberon, London, 1997

Hooray for Hollywood, Louisville, Kentucky, 19 February 1980

The London Cuckolds (after Edward Ravenscroft), Leicester Haymarket Theatre, May 1985; published London: Samuel French, 1986

Miracle on Wee Shona, BBC Radio Scotland, 2003

A Night at the Alex, BBC Radio Scotland, 1981

The Nitshill Writing Circle, Radio Scotland, 1984

Normal Service, Hampstead Theatre Club, London, March 1979; published by *Plays and Players*, May and June 1979; Royal Lyceum, Edinburgh, 1980; televised as BBC *Play for Today*, 1988

Nova Scotia, Traverse Theatre, Edinburgh, 25 April 2008; published London: Faber & Faber, 2008

The Slab Boys, Traverse Theatre, Edinburgh, 6 April 1978; televised for BBC *Play for Today*, 1979; text published Edinburgh: Scottish Society of Playwrights, 1981; revived as part 1 of *Paisley Patterns: The Slab Boys Trilogy*, Traverse, Edinburgh, May 1982; published in *The Traverse Plays 2*, Edinburgh: Salamander Press, 1997; film written and directed by Byrne, produced by Simon Relph and Lauren Lowenthal, 1997; filmscript published London: Faber & Faber, 1997; filmscript with introduction by Byrne, London: Faber & Faber, 2006;

Japanese translation performed and published by Tokyo Theatre Project, 2006; new production, Citizens Theatre, Glasgow and King's Theatre, Edinburgh, 2015

The Slab Boys Trilogy, performed as *Paisley Patterns: The Slab Boys Trilogy*, Traverse, Edinburgh, May 1982; published Harmondsworth: Penguin Books, 1987

Still Life, performed as part 3 of *Paisley Patterns: The Slab Boys Trilogy*, Traverse, Edinburgh 27 May 1982; published in *The Traverse Plays 4*, Edinburgh: Salamander Press

Tennis Elbow, audio drama (sequel to *Writer's Cramp*) broadcast on Sound Stage, Pitlochry Festival Theatre and Royal Lyceum Theatre, Edinburgh, 2021

The Three Sisters (after Chekhov), Tron Theatre, Glasgow, 2014

Tutti Frutti, broadcast by BBC1, 3 March–7 April 1987; book of the series published by London: BBC Books, 1987; performed National Theatre of Scotland/His Majesty's Theatre Aberdeen, 21 September 2006; playscript published London: Faber & Faber, 2006; original episodes re-broadcast BBC Scotland, 2019

Uncle Varick (after Chekhov), Royal Lyceum, Edinburgh, April 2004; new adaptation Royal Lyceum, Edinburgh, 2014

Underwood Lane, musical based on the Gerry Rafferty song catalogue, typescript, 2005; performed Johnstone Town Hall, 7–9 July 2022; performed Tron Theatre in a co-production with OneRen, Glasgow, 14–30 July 2022

Writer's Cramp, broadcast in shorter form as radio play, BBC Scotland, 1976; stage performance Calton Studios, Edinburgh, 22 August 1977; published in *Plays and Players*, December 1977; published in Alasdair Cameron (ed.) *Scot-Free: New Scottish Plays*, London: Nick Hern Books, 1990

Your Cheatin' Heart, broadcast BBC1, 11 October–15 November 1990; book of the series published London: BBC Books, 2001; published in Cairns Craig and Randall Stevenson (eds), *Twentieth-century Scottish Drama*, Edinburgh: Canongate

John Byrne